DISCOURSE FUNCTION
OF CONJOINERS
IN THE PASTORAL EPISTLES

DISCOURSE FUNCTION OF CONJOINERS IN THE PASTORAL EPISTLES

Jakob K. Heckert

Summer Institute of Linguistics

© 1991 by SIL International®
Library of Congress Catalog No: 2017961192
ISBN: 978-1-55671-439-9

Printed in the United States of America

No part of this publication may be reproduced, stored in a retrieval system, or transmitted in any form or by any means—electronic, mechanical, photocopy, recording, or otherwise—without the express permission of SIL International®. However, short passages, generally understood to be within the limits of fair use, may be quoted without written permission.

Copies of this and other publications of SIL International® may be obtained through distributors such as Amazon, Barnes & Noble, other worldwide distributors and, for select volumes, www.sil.org/resources/publications:

SIL International Publications
7500 W. Camp Wisdom Road
Dallas, Texas 75236-5629 USA

General inquiry: publications_intl@sil.org
Pending order inquiry: sales_intl@sil.org
www.sil.org/resources/publications

This book was produced from a digitally scanned reproduction of the original publication.

Cover Design
Barbara Alber

CONTENTS

Foreword by Stephen H. Levinsohn 7
Abbreviations 8

1 Introduction 9
   1.1 Basic function of particles 9
   1.2 The position of the particles 10
   1.3 The theoretical approach 10
   1.4 The texts used 11
   1.5 Authorship of the pastoral epistles 11
   1.6 Terminology 12
   1.7 Relationship between Classical and Koine Greek 12

2 Ἀλλά As a Marker of Contrast 13
   2.1 How traditional scholars of Classical Greek view ἀλλά 13
   2.2 How traditional scholars of New Testament Greek view ἀλλά 15
   2.3 How discourse linguists view ἀλλά in the New Testament 16
   2.4 The use of ἀλλά in the pastoral epistles 19
      2.4.1 When a negative marker precedes ἀλλά 19
      2.4.2 When a negative marker follows ἀλλά 22
      2.4.3 When there is no negative marker with ἀλλά 23
      2.4.4 The set construction οὐ μόνον ... ἀλλὰ καί 24
   2.5 When joined with some particle other than a negative 26
   2.6 Conclusion 28

3 Γάρ As a Marker of Confirmation 29
   3.1 How traditional scholars of Classical Greek view γάρ 29
   3.2 How traditional scholars of New Testament Greek view γάρ 30
   3.3 How discourse linguists view γάρ in the New Testament ... 31
   3.4 The use of γάρ in the pastoral epistles 32
   3.5 Conclusion 36

4 Δέ As a Marker of Development 37
   4.1 How traditional scholars of Classical Greek view δέ 37
   4.2 How traditional scholars of New Testament Greek view δέ 38
   4.3 How discourse linguists view δέ in the New Testament 40
   4.4 The use of δέ in the pastoral epistles 42
      4.4.1 Δέ as copulative 43
      4.4.2 The use of δέ to mark contrast 47
      4.4.3 The use of δέ in parenthetical constructions 49
   4.5 Special uses of δέ 51
      4.5.1 In set constructions 51
      4.5.2 Collocated with other particles 54

CONTENTS

4.5.3 The difference between δέ and ἀλλά 56
4.6 Conclusion 57

5 Adverbial Καί As a Marker of Addition 58
5.1 How traditional scholars of Classical Greek view the adverbial καί 58
5.2 How traditional scholars of New Testament Greek view the adverbial καί 59
5.3 How discourse linguists view the adverbial καί in the New Testament ... 60
5.4 The use of adverbial καί in the pastoral epistles 64
5.4.1 Same subject, different complement 64
5.4.2 Same subject, different verb 65
5.4.3 Different subject, same verb 66
5.4.4 Different subject, same predicate 67
5.4.5 The correlative καί . . . καί 68
5.4.6 The collocation of δέ with καί 69
5.5 Conclusion 70

6 Conjunctive Καί As a Marker of Addition 71
6.1 How traditional scholars of Classical Greek view καί 71
6.2. How traditional scholars of New Testament Greek view καί 73
6.3 How discourse linguists view καί in the New Testament 74
6.4 The use of the conjunctive καί in the pastoral epistles 75
6.4.1 The conjunctive καί between formally equal constituents 76
6.4.2 The conjunctive καί between formally unequal constituents 80
6.4.3 Καί in relation to the ellipsis of prepositions and determiners 82
6.4.4 The correlative καί . . . καί 86
6.5 Occurrences of καί that could be either adverbial or conjunctive 87
6.6 Conclusion 90

7 Οὖν As a Marker of Inference 91
7.1 How traditional scholars of Classical Greek view οὖν 91
7.2 How traditional scholars of New Testament Greek view οὖν 93
7.3 How discourse linguists view οὖν in the New Testament 94
7.4 The use of οὖν in the pastoral epistles 96
7.4.1 The inferential function of οὖν 96
7.4.2 The continuative function of οὖν 98
7.4.3 The function of οὖν when the previous context is introduced by γάρ 101
7.5 Conclusion 104

8 Conclusion 105

References 109

FOREWORD

It was my privilege, as an Adjunct Assistant Professor in the Summer Institute of Linguistics at the University of North Dakota, to supervise the research of Dr. Jakob Heckert into the discourse function of conjoiners in the Pastoral Epistles. Our interaction, first by correspondence and then face-to-face, deepened my appreciation for the need to bring together the insights of traditional scholarship into Classical and Koine Greek, an area in which Dr. Heckert was already an expert, and those of descriptive linguistics, especially recent advances in pragmatics and textlinguistics.

The reader of this volume will quickly come to appreciate Dr. Heckert's overviews of traditional descriptions, both in Classical and in Koine Greek, of the six conjoiners that feature most prominently in the Pastoral Epistles. These are followed by his evaluations of the conclusions reached by discourse linguists in the last two decades. Each chapter then demonstrates how the different pragmatic uses of the conjoiner concerned are rooted, nevertheless, in a single semantic function. A clear understanding of what this function is, and what its implications are in different contexts, enables us to appreciate how these conjoiners constrain and direct the development of the arguments of the Pastoral Epistles, on every occasion that they are used.

Stephen H. Levinsohn

ABBREVIATIONS

BAGD   Bauer, Arndt, Gingrich, Danker (1979)
BDR   Blass, Debrunner, Rehkopf (1976)
GNT   Greek New Testament (Aland et al. 1983)
KG   Kühner and Gerth (1955)
loc. cit. in the same place cited before
NASB   New American Standard Bible (1985)
RSV   Revised Standard Version (1973)

1 Introduction

As an instructor of Greek, I have long been concerned about conjoining particles in order to help my students understand the Greek text well and translate it properly. I did not, however, realize just how crucial they were for understanding and translating a text until I began research in this area in 1994.

Though I was already interested in discourse, since I was teaching a course in translation, what aroused my interest in conjunctions was Stephen Levinsohn's 1992 book, *Discourse Features of New Testament Greek*. Through his writing I came to realize what a great help these particles are for people who study and translate the Greek New Testament. The following statement from page 9 of his book encouraged me to make my own contribution to the endeavor on which he was working.

> It is my hope that, among those who use this book, there will be some who will want to investigate how the features described are used by the authors not covered. The result, in the not too distant future, I trust, will be a more comprehensive volume.

The result was that I read and studied materials in this area and finally decided to write my master's thesis on the topic of discourse conjoiners in the pastoral epistles.[1]

1.1 Basic function of particles

As I argue throughout this book, each of the particles considered here has a single basic function. These functions are as follows: ἀλλά is a marker of global contrast; γάρ introduces a proposition which usually confirms and strengthens an immediately preceding conjunct; δέ, a marker of development, either introduces a proposition that builds on a preceding conjunct and makes a contribution to the argument or, in the context of single or double difference contrast, marks a contrast (when no contrast is present, it is continuative); conjunctive καί is a marker of addition between two formally equal or unequal constituents; adverbial καί is a marker of addition across boundaries of propositions, constraining two constituents to parallel processing; οὖν marks inference and, in a context of resumption, continuation.

---

[1] This book is an adaptation of a thesis submitted to the graduate faculty of the University of North Dakota in partial fulfillment of the requirements for the degree of Master of Arts in 1994.

1.2 The position of the particles

Conjunctive καί and ἀλλά appear only between contiguous constituents, the former to associate two or more constituents together, the latter to contrast them globally. Adverbial καί usually does not begin a proposition, unless a post-positive conjunction also is present; it precedes the word, phrase, or clause which it constrains for parallel processing. All the other particles, viz. δέ, γάρ, and οὖν, are post-positive, that is, they never appear as the first word in their proposition. They are usually second, sometimes third, fourth, or even fifth, depending on the preceding word or grammatical construction. In pre-Classical Greek they were adverbs; and as adverbs, they modified the word immediately preceding them. When, in the course of language change, they became connective particles, they now joined together two constituents, but their conjunctive function was shaped by their adverbial orientation.

1.3 The theoretical approach

The basic approach I take to the function of the various particles is to consider each one as having one semantic function and two or more pragmatic uses. This notion is enunciated by Leech in his 1983 book, *Principles of Pragmatics*. He defines pragmatics as "the study of meaning in relation to speech situations" (p. 6). In pragmatics, meaning is not one but many, depending on the speech situation. Semantics looks at meaning from a dyadic perspective (what does X mean?) while pragmatics sees it in a triadic relationship (what did you mean by X?).

Leech rejects "semanticism" and "pragmaticism" and endorses the third alternative "complementarism." He states as follows the reason for his endorsement (p. 7): "Any account of meaning in language must (a) be faithful to the facts as we observe them, and (b) must be as simple and generalizable as possible." It is impossible to meet these criteria unless we combine semantics and pragmatics; only then can we achieve a satisfactory explanation.

The importance of what Leech says for my research of conjoiners lies in its implication. While the various uses of different particles need to be studied, it is important to generalize these and reduce them to one common function, if at all possible. The tendency of grammarians is to look at all of the Koine material and finish up with sometimes contradictory conclusions, because different authors tend to use particles in different ways. They fail to generalize sufficiently to simplify all the uses in one basic function. While each particle has different contextual effects (i.e., different uses), it also has inherent meaning (Levinsohn, personal communication).

This difference between one basic function and many uses appears to be espoused by Winer (1877:565):

> If then a conjunction is apparently used in a strange signification, we must first of all labour to show how in his thought the writer was led from the primary to the unusual meaning of the word. This, however, was never thought of; had it

been seriously considered, the chimera would at once have vanished into air. As purely fictitious as this carrot of "unlimited interchange" is the doctrine of "weakening" of conjunctions, which teaches that even particles with a sharply defined meaning, such as *for, but* are in many cases altogether redundant, or mere particles of transition.

1.4 The texts used

The Greek text that I use in this study is the 1983 GNT. While the glosses are my literal translation from the Greek text, the translation for each text comes from the Revised Standard Version unless otherwise indicated. The translations from the German and Greek of certain commentaries as well as other examples are my own. (I discovered that it was easier to place the Greek particles in their proper place when translating from the original than to use an English translation and add the Greek particles.)

1.5 Authorship of the pastoral Epistles

The Pauline authorship of the pastoral epistles is hotly contested. I cannot, therefore, avoid addressing the issue and taking a position. Nevertheless, since the Pauline authorship of the pastoral epistles is not my main concern, I have not investigated the matter thoroughly. I simply assume Pauline authorship for the pastoral epistles, quoting Edwards (1993) and Knight (1992) to substantiate my position.

The following comes from Edwards (1993:139):

> As a result of a careful examination, we find:
> 1. That the external evidence furnishes no ground to doubt the genuineness of the epistles;
> 2. That the difficulty of bringing the authorship of the epistles within the period of Paul's life, disappears on the theory of his second imprisonment in Rome; there is no adequate reason for not admitting this imprisonment;
> 3. That the internal peculiarities of the epistles, in regard to the subjects handled, the development of thought and mode of expression, show indeed some things of unusual character, but still not of a kind to have any decided weight against the genuineness; and
> 4. That it would be far more difficult to show, both in general and in particulars, how an impostor could have prepared three such epistles as these are, both in contents and in form, and foisted [them on the church] in the name of the Apostle Paul, than it is to prove their genuineness.

Knight (1992:52), after looking at all the problems raised by historical-critical scholarship, writes:

> Our conclusion is that the pastoral epistles were indeed written by the apostle Paul to his colleagues. This conclusion is based not only on the clear self-testimony of the letters to Paul as their author, their frequent personal references to Paul, their basic Pauline teaching, and their basic Pauline vocabulary

and style, but also on the satisfactory resolution of the perceived or real differences, which in the end point toward rather than away from that authorship.

1.6 Terminology

I use the terms *gloss* and *translation* in relation to a Greek word (a particle) in context; its reference may therefore vary, depending on the context in which the word is found. The term *meaning* has to do with the particle's basic gloss, while *use* refers to the activity of the word in a particular context. These are pragmatic designations, depending on the context. When I speak of *function*, I am thinking of the word's simple, generalizable use, the basic force of the particles (which for ἀλλά is contrast; for γάρ, confirmation; for δέ, development; for καί, addition; and for οὖν, inference).

I use the term *traditional scholar* of such people as lexicographers, grammarians, and philologists of both Classical and New Testament Greek. *Discourse linguists*, on the other hand, are people who are more oriented toward descriptive linguistics and discourse analysis.

1.7 Relationship between Classical and Koine Greek

Koine Greek, the Greek of the New Testament, must be understood primarily in terms of its Greek background. While Aramaic and Hebrew probably had a considerable impact on New Testament Greek, the basic functions of the conjoiners have generally carried over from those identified by Denniston (1954) for Classical Greek.

2 Ἀλλά As a Marker of Contrast

According to both traditional scholars and discourse linguists, ἀλλά has a sweep of functions, ranging from contradiction through opposition to limitation. There is a wide gap between the extremes of "elimination" and "balance," as Denniston calls them. Other functions of ἀλλά include its marking of transition, opposition, contrast, protest, difference, and objection. And these are just a few of those suggested by scholars.

My goal is to demonstrate that ἀλλά has only one basic function. All the others of its so-called functions are, in fact, only uses of the same basic function in different contexts.

To accomplish my goal, I (1) consider the functions of the conjunction as provided by traditional scholars of Classical Greek, (2) present a summary of traditional and discourse-linguistic research dealing with the various uses of ἀλλά in the New Testament, (3) evaluate the claims of these scholars, (4) test their findings against the uses of ἀλλά in the pastoral epistles, (5) investigate the particles associated with ἀλλά, and (6) present my conclusion.

2.1 How traditional scholars of Classical Greek view ἀλλά

Traditional scholars of Classical Greek claim that ἀλλά originated with the neuter plural of ἄλλος[1] (i.e., ἄλλα), meaning 'other things' and, when functioning as an adverb,[2] 'otherwise'. In view of this etymology we can assume that ἀλλά has to do with otherness, as Denniston (1954:1) points out: "The primary sense of 'otherness', diversity, contrast, runs through all the shades of meaning, from the strongest to the weakest." An understanding of this background provides us with a good starting point.

Liddell and Scott describe ἀλλά as a conjunction which functions adversatively to oppose, limit, or mark a transition for words, clauses, or sentences. They present (1940:67–68) two major uses of ἀλλά, the first being in relation to words and clauses, the second to sentences. The first major use they describe is opposition of single clauses, glossed 'but', when the preceding clause contains a negative marker. An example of this is in Homer's *Iliad* (15:690): Hector was not waiting, ἀλλά rushed forward. Frequently ἀλλά appears after οὐ μόνον or μὴ μόνον, as in Plato's *Phaedro* (228a): οὐ μόνον once, ἀλλά repeatedly. A variation of this use is as a limiting 'except, but', as in Sophocles's *Oedipus at Colonus* (241): no one jested ἀλλά I. In conditional sentences the apodosis is often introduced by ἀλλά, glossed 'yet, still, at least'; an example is in Homer's

---

[1] Meaning *other, another* (Liddell and Scott 1940:67).
[2] Neuter accusative singular and plural forms frequently function as adverbs.

Iliad (1.281). They also say that ἀλλά is used after a vocative in the same way as δέ,[3] as in Plato's *Euthyphro* (3C). (See chap. 4 for how ἀλλά differs from δέ.) It appears with a negative after an affirmative word or clause, translated by 'not', as in Plato's *Phaedro* (229d).

The second main use of ἀλλά described by Liddell and Scott (1940) is to oppose whole sentences. Glossed 'but, yet', it is frequently used in transitions (see Homer's *Iliad* 1.135). Homer repeatedly makes use of it in this way together with the imperative or subjunctive to remonstrate, encourage, or persuade: ἀλλ' ἴθι 'but go'; ἀλλ' ἄγε 'but come'; ἀλλὰ ἴωμεν 'but let us go' (Liddell and Scott 1889:37). After Homer it is used in questions and objections ('nay but...', 'well but...'), frequently with negatives, especially to raise and answer objections, as in Aristophanes's *Acharnians* (402, 407), and to affirm answers, as in Plato's *Protagoras* (330b). Authors make use of it to break off a subject abruptly, as in Homer's *Odysseus* (15:523): ἀλλά at any rate Zeus knows. Two other uses are to resume an address after a parenthesis, as in Pindar's *Olympian* (2:12, 4), and to mark elliptical phrases, as in Xenophon's *Cyrus* (1:4, 8): ἀλλά Cyrus remained upon it (the horse). It is apparent that in almost all of the preceding examples, ἀλλά forcefully contrasts the new with the previous material, giving listeners/readers notice that something unexpected is coming by which to make a point.

In summary, then, according to Liddell and Scott (1940) ἀλλά is a conjunction which functions adversatively to oppose (i.e., contrast), as in Homer's *Iliad* (15:690); to limit, as in Plato's *Phaedro* (228a); or to mark transition, as in Homer's *Iliad* (1.135) for words, clauses, or sentences.[4]

Smyth (1956:632) narrows the functions of ἀλλά from three to two, "exclusion" and "non-exclusion," though he indicates that it has a larger number of uses.[5] He notes that ἀλλά is "a strongly adversative conjunction (stronger than δέ)," connecting sentences, clauses, and single words (p. 633). He says that at times it need not or cannot be translated (but he gives no support for this claim). He points out that "ἀλλά marks opposition, contrast, protest, difference, objection, or limitation." Though I am not sure how to understand "marks," I take this to refer to uses rather than functions in the light of his remark about the two "notions" regarding ἀλλά, "exclusion" and "non-exclusion" (toleration). So opposition, contrast, protest, and objection would fall under the category of "opposition," while difference and limitation would come under the category of "limitation." While Smyth follows Liddell and

---

[3] A vocative may precede ἀλλά when a speaker turns from one person to another (Liddell and Scott 1897:327).

[4] Though in Liddell and Scott (1940) it is indicated that ἀλλά opposes words, no example is given. In the earlier edition (1897:63) only sentences and clauses are mentioned and its attachment to single words is described as "elliptical."

[5] The full statement reads, "It is thus used where one notion excludes another and where two notions are not mutually exclusive."

Scott in recognizing opposition and limitation, he has no category for Liddell and Scott's "transition."

Denniston (1954:1-6) narrows down the function of ἀλλά to the notion of "otherness," which runs through all the shades of meaning and manifests itself in "elimination," on the one hand, and "balance," on the other. He considers the conjunction an adversative connecting particle whose adversative force is usually strong; less frequently it is employed as a weaker (balancing) adversative. As he sees it, ἀλλά has three uses: (1) eliminative, substituting the true for the false; (2) balancing, sometimes answering a μέν in the preceding clause (in the main, a poetical use); and (3) oppositional, which is intermediate between the first two uses and occurs in a great many passages. Though at first glance Denniston's analysis does not seem helpful and, in fact, increases the number of possible functions, he does indicate that the primary sense of otherness runs through all the shades of meaning.

The basic function of ἀλλά in Classical Greek may thus be said to be otherness, even though this otherness manifests itself in many different ways, such as elimination, balance, and opposition (Denniston); opposition, contrast, protest, difference, objection, and limitation (Smyth); or opposition, limitation, and transition (Liddell and Scott).

The conclusions of these Classical Greek scholars point the way toward a unitary function of ἀλλά. Now we will look at how both traditional and discourse linguists describe the function of ἀλλά in the New Testament.

2.2 How traditional scholars of New Testament Greek view ἀλλά

BAGD (1979:38-39) in their summary statement for ἀλλά come up with two basic functions: "difference with or contrast to what precedes." But in their analysis they speak of four functions: contrast, transition (substantiated also by Moulton and Turner 1963:330), limitation, and intensification, apparently subdividing "difference with" into three. In their presentation, furthermore, they divide the uses of ἀλλά into *six* categories, which are as follows:

1. After a negative marker ἀλλά introduces contrast between clauses, as in Luke 20:38: God is not a God of the dead ἀλλά of the living. This, according to BDR (1976:378 [448:1]), is its most frequent use in the New Testament. In the combination 'not only . . . but also' (as in Rom. 1:32: οὐ μόνον do they do these things, ἀλλὰ καί they approve of others who do them), ἀλλά indicates ascensive force. Within clauses it contrasts a single word with a noun phrase, as in 1 Cor. 7:10: not I ἀλλά the Lord.
2. When whole clauses or larger units are compared, ἀλλά 'but, yet' indicates transition or contrast, as in Rom. 10:17-18: So then faith comes from hearing, δέ hearing comes through the word about Christ; ἀλλά I say, "Did Israel not hear?" It can introduce an objection, as in 1 Cor. 15:34c-35: I say this to your shame; ἀλλά someone will say, "How will the dead be raised?" Or it can introduce a limitation, as in Mark 14:36: Take this cup from me, ἀλλά not as I want.

3. Before independent clauses it marks the preceding as a settled matter, forming a transition to something new, as in 1 Cor. 10:19-20: What then shall we say, ... that an idol is something? ἀλλά what they sacrifice, they sacrifice to demons.
4. In the apodosis of conditional sentences ἀλλά can be translated 'yet, certainly, at least', as in 1 Cor. 8:6: just as there are many gods and many lords, ἀλλά to us there is one God, the Father.
5. Another function of ἀλλά is to indicate rhetorical intensification, 'not only this, but rather', as in 2 Cor. 7:11: for consider what zeal this divine sorrow worked for you, ἀλλά defense, ἀλλά indignation, ἀλλά fear, etc..
6. When collocated with an imperative or with ἵνα plus a subjunctive, ἀλλά strengthens the command and can be translated 'now, then', as in Acts 10:20: look, three men are seeking you, ἀλλά upon arising, go down.

BAGD conclude that ἀλλά is an adversative particle which indicates a difference with or a contrast to what precedes, whether on a clause or sentence level. These functions are compatible to those of Liddell and Scott, "oppose" and "limit," and of Smyth, "exclusive" and "non-exclusive."

2.3 How discourse linguists view ἀλλά in the New Testament

Discourse linguists improve on the traditional view that ἀλλά has two basic functions, viz. opposition and limitation, and an underlying notion of otherness. For example, Poythress (1984), in his study of John's Gospel, provides a number of uses of ἀλλά, viz. contrast, counter expectation, intensification, and contradiction. While he does not say anything about a basic function, he appears to consider contrast to be basic. Poythress comes to the conclusion that ἀλλά separates two contrasting sentences whose meaning is virtually identical except that one is negated, as in John 15:16: you did not choose me, ἀλλά I chose you. He further claims that ἀλλά introduces counterexpectation, as in John 11:42: Moreover, I know that you hear me constantly, ἀλλά because of the crowd around me I said, "Father, I thank you that you heard me.".

Poythress notes two additional uses in John, for both of which the presence of ἀλλά presupposes additional information. First, he says that John uses ἀλλά for intensification, introducing statements that heighten the preceding proposition, as in John 16:2: they will throw you out of the synagogue, ἀλλά the hour will come that everyone who kills you will presume to worship God. This example is similar to those in which οὐ μόνον ... ἀλλά καί is used with ascensive force (see sec. 2.5): not only will they throw you out of the synagogue, but the hour will also come ... (see especially 2 Tim. 4:8, which is discussed in sec. 2.5). Poythress's second additional use of ἀλλά in John involves two statements contrasted to the point of contradiction. An example of this is in John 15:20a–21: If they kept my word, they also will keep your word; ἀλλά all these things they do to you because of my name. Here the presence of ἀλλά presupposes the truth of the opposite of the hypothetical situation described in the preceding sentence: ἀλλά because they have kept neither my word nor yours, they will do these things.

In summary, it can be said that all four of Poythress's uses of ἀλλά involve the contradiction of some previous assumption or expectation. This is similar to the οὐ μόνον ... ἀλλὰ καί construction (sec. 2.4.4), which involves contradiction by correction.

Now we will consider the view of Regina Blass, another discourse linguist. Blass (1993) looks at the New Testament text from the perspective of relevance theory. She claims that ἀλλά has a dual function, constraining to contradict and to confirm. Though it may seem that she is proposing two functions of ἀλλά, upon closer inspection one finds that she indeed claims a double function: the conjunction constrains to contradict and confirm at the same time.

According to Blass, in one sense ἀλλά does not function any differently from *but* in English. Both "establish the inferential relation of contradiction between a proposition R (i.e., the rejected proposition) and the proposition they introduce and all give rise to the contextual effect of elimination" (p. 19). But there is an aspect to the function of ἀλλά, as she sees it, which differentiates it from *but* in English: the former provides backwards confirmation (i.e., it strengthens or confirms the previous conjunct), but the latter does not. She concludes that ἀλλά "not only constrains to contradict something but also to confirm and strengthen something" (p. 22).

Thus Blass claims that ἀλλά has a dual function; it constrains to confirm the previous proposition and to contradict the underlying assumption. An example is seen in Rom. 2:13:

> For it is οὐ (not) the hearers of the law who are righteous before God,
> ἀλλά (but) the doers of the law who will be justified.

She holds that underlying the first conjunct in this text is assumption R, 'For it is the hearers of the law who are righteous before God.' With a negation the Romans text denies this. The second conjunct introduced by ἀλλά confirms this denial and thereby eliminates the assumption.

While the basic function of ἀλλά is contrastive, an important factor in its interpretation is the presence and the position of a negative marker such as οὐ. Blass (1993:18) claims that, when ἀλλά is preceded by a negative marker, as in Rom. 2:13, the first assumption which the hearer is presumed to hold is denied and a second one is put in its place. The conjunction provides the answer to the question implied by the negation and corrects the hearer's misconception. An illustration of this is in Rom. 3:27:

> Where then is boasting? It is excluded. Through what law? Of works?
> Οὐχί, ἀλλά (not so, but) through the law of faith).

The negative οὐ(χί) negates the assumption that the 'law of works' prevents boasting. What prevents boasting instead, Paul claims, is the 'law of faith'.

The negation does not have to cover the whole proposition; it can be partial. To accomplish this, the construction οὐ μόνον ... ἀλλά (plus or minus καί) is often used. As Blass states (p. 20), "What is to be eliminated is the truth-conditional content of what 'only' contributes to the proposition, nothing else." The proposition introduced by ἀλλά is not primarily a correction of the previous conjunct but an addition to it. The adverbial καί, which may or may not be present (but is usually present in the New Testament examples), constrains to processing this conjunct in parallel (see sec. 5.1) with the conjunct associated with οὐ μόνον. The two are joined to form a new conclusion. An example is Rom. 4:16: οὐ μόνον out of the law αλλὰ καί out of the faith of Abraham. Since readers could come to the conclusion that the promise discussed previously was only for the physical descendants of Abraham ('out of the law'), Paul precluded this by using οὐ μόνον in the first proposition followed by a second with ἀλλά to make the correction. The conclusion is that all those who believe like Abraham, whether physical descendants or not, are heirs of the promise. This kind of process, according to Blass (p. 20), is an activity of backwards confirmation (i.e., a reference to the previous constituent which is corrected and expanded) and strengthening. She calls this a "construction of correction" (p. 9).

A negative marker can be used not only before, but also after, ἀλλά. In this context, Blass points out, "ἀλλά is designed to deny some expectation which the speaker takes the hearer to have drawn from the preceding conjunct" (p. 21). A good example of this is 2 Tim. 2:9: For which I suffer even imprisonment as an evil-doer. Ἀλλά the word of God is not bound. (See the discussion of this verse in sec. 2.4.2.)

When ἀλλά is used in the absence of a negation, it introduces a counter-expectation. That is, the contrasted constituent introduced by ἀλλά counters the expectations raised by the preceding conjunct. There are especially striking cases of such constructions in the Gospel of John, as in John 16:20: you will be sorrowful, ἀλλά your sorrow shall be turned into joy. Paul too uses this kind of construction in his epistles, as in 2 Cor. 4:16: even if our outer person is destroyed, ἀλλά our inward person is renewed day by day.

Though Blass considers backwards confirmation and strengthening to be an inherent part of the function of ἀλλά, I find no evidence of this when the conjunction is used in the absence of negation. For example, in John 16:20, the purpose of the conjunct 'your sorrow shall be turned into joy' is surely not to strengthen the previous proposition ('you will be sorrowful'), but to introduce the hope of later joy (see 1 Tim. 1:13, 15–16).

I therefore conclude that, although the proposition introduced by ἀλλά does strengthen the previous proposition in the context of negation, strengthening is not an inherent part of the function of ἀλλά. Rather it contrasts a previous assumption or expectation for the purpose of elimination, denial, or correction. It could be called a marker of global contrast, since the contrast is not one or more points of difference within a proposition, that is, not Dooley's (1993:45) single or double difference contrast, but between one proposition and a second one (Poythress 1984:321).

2.4 The use of ἀλλά in the pastoral Epistles

The conjunction ἀλλά appears twenty-five times in the pastoral epistles. In seventeen of these instances it is preceded by a negative; in three, a negative follows; in two, there is no negative; and three times it appears in a limiting οὐ μόνον... ἀλλὰ καί construction (macBible 1988).

Here in section 2.4 I will demonstrate that the basic function of the adversative particle ἀλλά in the pastoral epistles is to mark global contrast, although this function may be modified to a degree, depending on the presence or absence of a negative marker and its position in relation to ἀλλά. Even in the set construction οὐ μόνον... ἀλλὰ καί, ἀλλά functions contrastively within the limits set by οὐ μόνον, on the one hand, and καί, on the other.

2.4.1 When a negative marker precedes ἀλλά

That ἀλλά is a contrast marker will be shown by examples from several different contexts: ἀλλά preceded by a negative (sec. 2.4.1), followed by a negative (sec. 2.4.2), and in the absence of a negative (sec. 2.4.3).

In the majority of its occurrences, the conjunction ἀλλά is found in a context in which a negative marker (μή or οὐ) or compounds thereof precede it. This may be considered the unmarked relationship.[6] Unless the context determines otherwise, it is the "rejected" proposition, the one preceding ἀλλά, that is to be replaced by the one which follows it. In other words, ἀλλά contrasts the rejected proposition with the one which replaces it. Several examples of this follow.

1 Tim. 4:12a μηδείς σου τῆς νεότητος καταφρονείτω,
no-one of-you the youth let-despise

'Let no one despise your youth'

12b ἀλλὰ τύπος γίνου τῶν πιστῶν
ἀλλά pattern be of-the believers

ἐν λόγῳ, ἐν ἀναστροφῇ, ἐν ἀγάπῃ
in word in conduct in love

ἐν πίστει, ἐν ἁγνείᾳ.
in faith in purity

'but set the believers an example in speech and conduct, in love, in faith, in purity.'

In 1 Tim. 4:12 the negative precedes ἀλλά; ἀλλά occurs between two clause constituents, μηδείς σου τῆς νεότητος καταφρονείτω 'let no one despise your

---

[6] This extensive association is present not only in the pastoral epistles but in the New Testament in general (BDR 1976:378) and apparently even in Classical Greek literature (Liddell and Scott 1940:67).

youth',[7] on the one hand, and τύπος γίνου τῶν πιστῶν ἐν λόγῳ, κτλ. 'be an example for believers in word, etc.', on the other. Here Paul directs Timothy not to think lightly of himself because he is only in his thirties. Instead, he urges him to think of himself as a model for believers in his conduct and faith. Knight (1992:205) describes the proposition introduced by ἀλλά as an "antidote" to Timothy's fear of other people's opinion of him. Thus there is a global contrast between the way Timothy could act and how Paul encourages him to act (see also 2 Tim. 4:16).

Another example is seen in 1 Tim. 3:3:

1 Tim. 3:3a μὴ πάροινον,   μὴ πλήκτην,
         not addicted-to-wine not striker

3b **ἀλλὰ** ἐπιεικῆ, ἄμαχον, ἀφιλάργυρον,
   ἀλλά   gentle peaceful content

'no drunkard, not violent, but gentle, not quarrelsome, and no lover of money.'

The context of 1 Tim. 3:3 deals with the qualifications for overseers. The δεῖ εἶναι (it is necessary to be) construction from v. 2 continues into v. 3. Leaders of God's people are not (μή) to be addicted to wine nor to be bullies. Instead (ἀλλά) they are to be gentle, peaceful, and content. The conjunction "ἀλλά 'but' after the negative indicates the positive contrast afforded by ἐπιεικῆ" (Knight 1992:160). It contrasts the characteristics which are to be rejected with others which are to replace them (see also 2 Tim. 1:7).

1 Tim. 6:17a Τοῖς πλουσίοις ἐν τῷ νῦν αἰῶνι παράγγελλε
             to-the rich   in the now   age   command

μὴ ὑψηλοφρονεῖν **μηδὲ** ἠλπικέναι ἐπὶ πλούτου ἀδηλότητι,
not to-be-proud   nor   to-hope   upon riches uncertain

'As for the rich in this world, charge them not to be haughty, nor to set their hopes on uncertain riches'

17b **ἀλλ'** ἐπὶ θεῷ τῷ παρέχοντι ἡμῖν πάντα
    ἀλλά   upon God who provides us   all-things

πλουσίως εἰς ἀπόλαυσιν.
richly   for enjoyment

'but on God who richly furnishes us with everything to enjoy.'

The rich were tempted to consider their wealth as an indication of their greater worth (ὑψηλοφρονεῖν 'to be proud'). Paul urges them through Timothy not to hope on the uncertainty of riches (ἠλπικέναι ἐπὶ πλούτου ἀδηλότητι). Instead

---

[7] BAGD (1979:420) has "Let no one look down on you because you are young" (This is a matter of attitude on Timothy's part and not a matter of controlling other people's actions.

he encourages them to set their hope on God. The words ἀλλ' ἐπὶ θεῷ 'but on God' are a forceful statement, in contrast to ἐπὶ πλούτου ἀδηλότητι concerning the one on whom the rich should set their hope (Knight 1992:273). Here ἀλλά contrasts the rejected object of hope with the one that is to replace it (see also 1 Tim. 2:12).

The next example is somewhat different:

2 Tim. 4:16a Ἐν τῇ πρώτῃ μου ἀπολογίᾳ **οὐδείς** μοι παρεγένετο,
in the first of-me defense <u>οὐδείς</u> me was-with

'At my first defense no one took my part;'

16b **ἀλλὰ** πάντες με ἐγκατέλιπον·
<u>ἀλλά</u> all me left-behind;

'all deserted me.'

In 2 Tim. 2:16 Paul says that at his preliminary investigation (πρώτη ἀπολογία) not even a single person (οὐδείς) came to his aid. In this context the proposition rejected in 16a is not replaced by a different one; rather, the conjuncts linked by ἀλλά make the same point, thereby strengthening and intensifying the impact (BAGD, Poythress 1984). Here ἀλλά contrasts οὐδείς μοι παρεγένετο 'no one was with me' (as could be expected) in 16a with πάντες με ἐγκατέλιπον 'all left me' (see also 1 Tim. 4:12).

In the context of the following example, the contrast is not a contradiction but a correction:

1 Tim. 5:23a **Μηκέτι** ὑδροπότει,
no-longer drink-water

'no longer drink only water,'

23b **ἀλλὰ** οἴνῳ ὀλίγῳ χρῶ διὰ τὸν στόμαχον
<u>ἀλλά</u> wine little use because-of the stomach

καὶ τὰς πυκνάς σου ἀσθενείας.
and the frequent of-you weaknesses

'but use a little wine for the sake of your stomach and your frequent ailments.'

Here Paul's concern about his companion's health moved him to urge Timothy to drink no longer water only (ὑδροπότει), but in contrast (ἀλλά) Timothy is urged to use a little wine (οἴνῳ ὀλίγῳ χρῶ), the reason being given in the διά phrase (Knight 1992:240). (This is similar to the construction οὐ μόνον ... ἀλλὰ δέ.) This understanding is inherent in the context (in the modifier ὀλίγῳ 'little'), not in the conjunction proper. Thus the observation made by traditional linguists about ἀλλά being an introducer of limitation or correction is exemplified in the pastoral epistles.

In summary, when a negative marker precedes ἀλλά, the proposition it introduces usually replaces the prior conjunct. When this is not the case, the effects of "intensification" (BAGD, Poythress 1984) and "limitation" (Liddell and Scott) are produced. Nevertheless, even in this context, ἀλλά is always used to contrast the proposition it introduces with a previously rejected one.

2.4.2 When a negative marker follows ἀλλά

There are only three examples found in the pastoral epistles in which a negative marker follows ἀλλά. In these passages the negative particle does not so much cancel as correct an expectation. All three of the examples are in 2 Timothy:

2 Tim. 1:12a δι' ἣν αἰτίαν καὶ ταῦτα πάσχω,
for this reason also these I-suffer
'and therefore I suffer as I do.'

12b ἀλλ' οὐκ ἐπαισχύνομαι,
ἀλλά οὐκ I-am-ashamed
'But I am not ashamed,'

Paul knows that he is suffering imprisonment and other experiences (καὶ ταῦτα) because (δι' ἣν αἰτίαν 'for which reason, wherefore' [Knight 1992:378]) he is a herald, an apostle, and a teacher of the gospel. Although it might be expected that he would be ashamed of the stigma of being imprisoned, ἀλλά οὐκ in 2 Tim. 1:12b corrects this expectation. He is not ashamed.

The second example is in 2 Tim. 2:9, where again the negative follows ἀλλά:

2 Tim. 2:9a ἐν ᾧ κακοπαθῶ μέχρι δεσμῶν ὡς κακοῦργος,
in which I-suffered until bonds as evildoer
'for which I am suffering and wearing fetters like a criminal.'

9b ἀλλὰ ὁ λόγος τοῦ θεοῦ οὐ δέδεται.
ἀλλά the word of-the God not is-bound
'But the word of God is not fettered.'

Paul's imprisonment could mean that his proclamation of the good news had ceased. He rejects such a natural expectation because of his trust in the power of God's word. He may be chained in prison, but the word which he proclaims is not chained (ἀλλὰ ὁ λόγος τοῦ θεοῦ οὐ δέδεται), as *he* is. It goes out among people and reaches all whom God wishes to reach. Here ἀλλά introduces a proposition that corrects the expectation activated by the preceding clause; in contrast (ἀλλά) to his imprisonment, Paul vigorously asserts that "the word of God is not imprisoned" (Knight 1992:398).

The third example is in 2 Tim. 3:8:

2 Tim. 3:8 ὃν τρόπον δὲ Ἰάννης καὶ Ἰαμβρῆς ἀντέστησαν Μωϋσεῖ
which way but Jannes and Jambres resisted Moses

οὕτως καὶ οὗτοι ἀνθίστανται τῇ ἀληθείᾳ,
so also these resist the truth

ἄνθρωποι κατεφθαρμένοι τὸν νοῦν, ἀδόκιμοι περὶ τὴν πίστιν
people destroying the mind untested about the faith

'As Jannes and Jambres opposed Moses, so these men also oppose the truth, men of corrupt mind and counterfeit faith;'

9 **ἀλλ' οὐ** προκόψουσιν ἐπὶ πλεῖον,
ἀλλά not advance to more

ἡ γὰρ ἄνοια αὐτῶν ἔκδηλος ἔσται πᾶσιν,
the for ignorance of-them evident will-be to-all

ὡς καὶ ἡ ἐκείνων ἐγένετο.
as also the of-those was

'but they will not go very far, for their folly will be plain to all, as was that of those two men.'

The future of false teachers may well appear promising. Their own expectations as well as those of other people are that they will succeed. Nevertheless in 2 Tim. 3:8, Paul expresses his certainty that they will *not* (ἀλλ' οὐ προκόψουσιν ἐπὶ πλεῖον); God will expose their ignorance, so that they will fail miserably. Their expectation of success is corrected with the proposition introduced by ἀλλά.

Thus, in each of these three examples, ἀλλά introduces a contrast with the preceding proposition while the negative marker which follows contrasts with and corrects an expectation raised in the first conjunct.

2.4.3 When there is no negative marker with ἀλλά

The conjunction ἀλλά occurs without a negative only twice in the pastoral epistles. In these two examples there is a negative situation preceding ἀλλά instead of a negative *marker*. The conjunction ἀλλά introduces a correction of the expectation created by the first conjunct; an incorrect expectation is canceled and a proper expectation is put in its place.

1 Tim. 1:13a τὸ πρότερον ὄντα βλάσφημον καὶ διώκτην καὶ ὑβριστήν·
the formerly being blasphemer and persecutor and proud-person

'though I formerly blasphemed, persecuted and insulted him;'

13b **ἀλλὰ** ἠλεήθην,
ἀλλά I-received-mercy

ὅτι ἀγνοῶν ἐποίησα ἐν ἀπιστίᾳ.
because being-ignorant I-acted in unbelief

'but I received mercy because I had acted ignorantly in unbelief,'

As a blasphemer, persecutor, and insolent person Paul could not expect any mercy from God. The 13b proposition introduced by ἀλλά corrects the normal expectation of 13a. Contrary to what Paul could expect, God was merciful to him because Paul had acted in unbelief. God brought him to faith in Jesus Christ. The contrast is between Paul's expectation of judgment because of his unbelief and God's grace manifested in Jesus Christ through the gospel. Knight (1992:95) states, "ἀλλά indicates a contrast to what precedes and provides the appropriate abrupt turning point."

1 Tim. 1:15 πιστὸς ὁ λόγος καὶ πάσης ἀποδοχῆς ἄξιος,
faithful the saying and of-all acceptance worthy

ὅτι Χριστὸς Ἰησοῦς ἦλθεν εἰς τὸν κόσμον
that Christ Jesus came into the world

ἁμαρτωλοὺς σῶσαι· ὧν πρῶτός εἰμι ἐγώ,
sinners to-save of-which first I-am myself

'The saying is sure and worthy of full acceptance, that Christ Jesus came into the world to save sinners. And I am the foremost of sinners;'

16 ἀλλὰ διὰ τοῦτο ἠλεήθην,
ἀλλά because-of this I-received-mercy

ἵνα ἐν ἐμοὶ πρώτῳ ἐνδείξηται
so-that in me as-first might-display

Χριστὸς Ἰησοῦς τὴν ἅπασαν μακροθυμίαν,
Christ Jesus the all patience

πρὸς ὑποτύπωσιν τῶν μελλόντων
for example of-the coming

πιστεύειν ἐπ' αὐτῷ εἰς ζωὴν αἰώνιον.
to-believe on him for life eternal

'but I received mercy for this reason, that in me, as the foremost, Jesus Christ might display his perfect patience for an example to those who were to believe in him for eternal life.'

In 1 Tim. 1:15 no negative particle is present. Two conjuncts are crucial here, ἁμαρτωλοὺς ... ὧν πρῶτός εἰμι ἐγώ 'sinners, of whom I am the first' and ἠλεήθην 'I received mercy'. A sinner can expect judgment not mercy, and all the more as 'chief of sinners'. Yet Paul received mercy, which is contrary to human expectation. Knight (1992:103) writes, "Paul again ... contrasts (ἀλλά) to it [his sinfulness] the mercy of Christ."

2.4.4 The set construction οὐ μόνον ... ἀλλὰ καί

The construction οὐ μόνον ... ἀλλὰ καί appears three times in the pastoral epistles. As already noted in section 2.3, Blass (1993:20) suggests that this "construction of correction" eliminates the assumption associated with μόνον 'only', while the conjunct introduced by ἀλλά adds further information not part of the previous proposition. The presence of καί, in turn, indicates that the new constituent is to be added to the previous one: it "introduces a constraint of parallel processing" (loc. cit.).

The following is the first example:

2 Tim. 2:20a Ἐν μεγάλῃ δὲ οἰκίᾳ **οὐκ** ἔστιν
in great but house <u>οὐκ</u> is

μόνον σκεύη χρυσᾶ καὶ ἀργυρᾶ
<u>μόνον</u> vessels golden and silver

'In a great house there are not only vessels of gold and silver'

20b **ἀλλὰ καὶ** ξύλινα καὶ ὀστράκινα
<u>ἀλλὰ</u> <u>καὶ</u> wooden and earthen

καὶ ἃ μὲν εἰς τιμὴν ἃ δὲ εἰς ἀτιμίαν.
and which on-the-one-hand for honor which but for dishonor

'but also of wood and earthenware, and some for noble use, some for ignoble use.'

The construction οὐ μόνον... ἀλλὰ καί eliminates the assumption Ἐν μεγάλῃ δὲ οἰκίᾳ... ἔστιν μόνον σκεύη χρυσᾶ καὶ ἀργυρᾶ 'in a great house are only vessels of silver and gold'. It also joins to the previous proposition as corrected by the elimination of μόνον 'only' the additional conjunct ξύλινα καὶ ὀστράκινα 'wooden and earthen (vessels)'. The point is that a royal (great) household contains both kinds of vessels, those made of precious metal and those made of common material. The adverbial καί marks that which is being added to the items present in the previous conjunct (Blass 1993:9).

The second example is 2 Tim. 4:8:

2 Tim. 4:8a λοιπὸν ἀπόκειταί μοι ὁ τῆς δικαιοσύνης στέφανος,
finally laid-up for-me the of-the righteousness crown

ὃν ἀποδώσει μοι ὁ κύριος ἐν ἐκείνῃ τῇ ἡμέρᾳ,
which will-give to-me the Lord in that the day

ὁ δίκαιος κριτής,
the righteous judge

'Henceforth there is laid up for me the crown of righteousness, which the Lord the righteous judge will award to me on that Day,'

8b **οὐ μόνον** δὲ ἐμοὶ
<u>οὐ</u> <u>μόνον</u> but to-me

'and not only to me'

8c ἀλλὰ καὶ πᾶσι τοῖς ἠγαπηκόσι τὴν ἐπιφάνειαν αὐτοῦ.
ἀλλὰ καὶ to-all the loving the appearance of-him
'but also to all who have loved his appearing.'

Here the phrase οὐ μόνον ... ἀλλὰ καί functions the same way as in the previous example. It eliminates the assumption 'the Lord will give the crown of righteousness only to me' and singles out πᾶσι τοῖς ἠγαπηκόσι τὴν ἐπιφάνειαν αὐτοῦ 'to those who love his appearing' for parallel processing with ἐμοί 'to me'. Both Paul and all of God's people will receive the crown of life. Knight (1992:462) writes, "The ascensive force of ἀλλὰ καί gathers up those specified after it and includes them with the one specified by οὐ μόνον."

What is different about 2 Tim. 4:8 is that δέ appears right after οὐ μόνον. While it does not change the overall function of the phrase, it adds another dimension to it; that is, it performs a transitional function in this context. It marks development by building on the previous proposition (Paul will receive the crown of life) and by making a distinct contribution to the argument (all Christians will receive the crown of life). The adverbial καί supports the development as it joins πᾶσι τοῖς ἠγαπηκόσι to ἐμοί.

Thus I conclude that in the set construction οὐ μόνον ... ἀλλὰ καί, ἀλλά does not lose its basic contrastive function. The contrast, however, is restricted to eliminating the assumption associated with μόνον and expanding the boundary μόνον had set by adding a new conjunct. The καί marks a phrase following καί for parallel processing with a pronoun preceding it. The basic function of ἀλλά is not altered by being in a "set" construction.

2.5 When joined with some particle other than a negative

When ἀλλά is collocated with some particle other than the negative, it still retains its contrastive function. (Liddell and Scott and BAGD point this out.) The following are some collocations of ἀλλά with a non-negative particle in Classical Greek: (1) Homer used ἀλλ' ἄρα in transitions (Homer's *Iliad* 6:418); later it was used to introduce objections (as in Plato's *Apology* 25a) and also to introduce questions. (2) The combination ἀλλ' οὖν meant 'but then, however' (as in Herodotus 3:140); it was also concessive, 'at all events' (as in Aristophanes's *Ranae* 58:948). (3) The combination ἀλλὰ γάρ, frequently with words between ἀλλά and γάρ meant 'but really, certainly' (in Euripides's *Phoenissae* 1308). (4) The combination ἀλλ' ἤ was used in questions, chiefly in surprise or remonstrance (in Plato's *Georgias* 447a). There are other words as well found in Classical Greek following ἀλλά, such as τοι, μέντοι, μήν, γε, and δή (Liddell and Scott 1940:68); they only strengthen it. As Liddell and Scott point out when ἀλλά joins with other particles, each one retains its proper force.

In the New Testament, too, particles other than the negative are joined with ἀλλά. When ἀλλά is combined with καί 'also', γε 'indeed, certainly', οὐδέ, 'not, not even', and μενοῦν γε 'rather, on the contrary', contrast is always present. (The following examples are in Pauline, but not in the pastoral epistles.)

2 Cor. 11:1a Ὄφελον ἀνείχεσθε μου μικρόν
I-wish you-were-enduring of-me little
'I wish you would bear with me

τι ἀφροσύνης·
something of-foolishness
in a little foolishness.'

1b **ἀλλά καί** ἀνέχεσθέ μου.
ἀλλά καί endure of-me
'Do also bear with me.'[8]

In 2 Cor. 11:1 ἀλλά introduces a positive counterpoint. Paul commands the Corinthians to put up also with his foolishness as they do with that of others (see 10:12, 18).

1 Cor. 9:2a εἰ ἄλλοις οὐκ εἰμὶ ἀπόστολος,
if to-others not I-am apostle
'if to others I am not an apostle-'

2b **ἀλλά γε** ὑμῖν εἰμι·
ἀλλά γε to-you I-am
'but I am at least to you.'[9]

In 1 Cor. 9:2b Paul, with ἀλλά, corrects the possible expectation prompted by 2a. It is not true that he is an apostle to no one; at least he is an apostle to the Corinthians.

Gal. 2:2b κατ' ἰδίαν δὲ τοῖς δοκοῦσιν,
privately but to-the important

μή πως εἰς κενὸν τρέχω ἢ ἔδραμον.
lest somehow for nothing I-am-running or did-run
'but privately before those who were of repute . . . lest somehow I should be running or had run in vain.'

3a **ἀλλ' οὐδὲ** Τίτος ὁ σὺν ἐμοί,
ἀλλ' οὐδέ Titus the with me

Ἕλλην ὤν, ἠναγκάσθη περιτμηθῆναι·
Greek being was-forced to-be-circumcised
'But even Titus who, was with me, was not compelled to be circumcised, though he was a Greek.'

---

[8] The translation is my own (cf. RSV).
[9] The translation is my own (cf. BDR 1976:364–65).

Here in Gal. 2:2 Paul corrects an expectation that the leaders in the church at Jerusalem would insist that Titus, a Greek, be circumcised.

Phil. 3:7b ταῦτα ἥγημαι διὰ τὸν Χριστὸν ζημίαν.
these I-consider because-of the Christ trash

'[Whatever gain I had] I counted as loss for the sake of Christ.'

8a ἀλλὰ μενοῦνγε καὶ ἡγοῦμαι πάντα ζημίαν εἶναι
ἀλλὰ μενοῦνγε also consider all trash to-be

'Indeed I count everything as loss.'

With the use of ἀλλά, Paul eliminates any doubt that he considers ταῦτα in 7b as ζημίαν 'trash'. Indeed (μενοῦνγε, see BDR 1976:366) he regards πάντα 'all things' as 'trash'.

Thus ἀλλά in collocation with any of these other particles still has its basic contrastive function.

2.6 Conclusion

In the preceding sections it has been demonstrated that the basic function of ἀλλά is contrast although in each of its occurrences the context determines the specific use of the conjunction. Thus, when a negative marker *precedes* ἀλλά, the second conjunct replaces a rejected proposition; when a negative marker *follows* ἀλλά the expectations raised by the preceding conjunct are denied; and when a negative marker is absent, the second proposition corrects the expectations initiated by the first one. Moreover, when ἀλλά appears in the set construction οὐ μόνον ... ἀλλὰ καί, it also corrects something.

3 Γάρ As a Marker of Confirmation

The purpose of this chapter is to delimit the basic function of the conjunctive γάρ, which has been variously described as confirmatory, causal, explanatory, connective, assentient, etc. In the sections of this chapter it will be demonstrated that the basic function of γάρ is *confirmation*. All other uses are derived from this basic function.

3.1 How traditional scholars of Classical Greek view γάρ

According to Classical Greek scholars γάρ has a double orientation, functioning both as an adverb and as a conjunction. Schwyzer and Debrunner (1950, vol. 2, p. 560), together with other scholars of Classical Greek (see Denniston 1954:56, Liddell and Scott 1940:338, and Smyth 1956:638), maintain that γάρ is the result of a "crasis" between γέ 'at any rate, indeed' and ἄρα 'then, therefore' and that this is the reason for its dual function as conjunction and adverb.

The adverbial orientation, which was first, is glossed 'in fact, indeed'. The conjunctive orientation followed; it is glossed 'for'. (Note that although γάρ functioned as an adverb in Classical Greek, by the time of the New Testament the adverbial orientation had apparently disappeared, it was used only as a conjunction in the New Testament.) Eventually, as a conjunction, γάρ came to have two basic functions, the earlier confirmatory and causal, and the second, somewhat later, explanatory, which was "nearly related to the confirmatory" (Denniston 1954:56).

Liddell and Scott (1940:338) say that γάρ 'for' is a causal conjunction used alone or with some particle to introduce the cause or reason of what precedes (in Homer's *Iliad* 1.56). By inversion it precedes the proposition to which it relates, explaining it; used in this way it is translated 'since, as' (in Herodotus 1.8). It sometimes appears in elliptical phrases in which that for which γάρ gives the reason is not explicitly stated (in Plato's *Symposium* 194a). It is used in abrupt questions which can be translated as 'what, why' (in Homer's *Iliad* 18.182). It also shows up together with an optative[1] to strengthen a wish (in Euripides's *Cyclops* 261).

Often γάρ is joined with ἀλλά (in Aeschylus's *Septem contra Thebas* 861), ἄρα (Plato's *Protagoras* 315d), δή (Herodotus 1.34), οὖν (Homer's *Iliad* 15.232), and other such words. In each case γάρ retains its causal function.

According to Liddell and Scott, then, the function of γάρ is primarily causal. It maintains its causal function even when it is used with some particle or other conjunction. It is surprising that Liddell and Scott make no mention of the

---

[1] One function of the optative in the main clause is 'wish'. The other is 'potential'.

adverbial orientation of γάρ. Smyth (1954:638), on the other hand, describes three uses—the elliptical, abrupt questions, and wish—as adverbial.

Denniston (1954:56-114) provides some insight into the historical development of γάρ from an adverb of asseveration (i.e., a strong assertion) to a confirmatory and causal use, translated 'for', saying "it is unlikely that 'for' is the primary meaning" (p. 57), since few connecting particles were originally conjunctions. Therefore, the "connective force" or "causal sense" followed after and developed from the asseverative force of γάρ. Since the asseverative force is limited, and since "inferential" has no claim to recognition (p. 57), Denniston takes the basic function to be confirmatory and causal, "giving the ground for belief or the motive for action." He considers the explanatory function to be "nearly related to the confirmatory" (p. 58) and γάρ thus to have an adverbial and a conjunctive orientation, the latter functioning in a confirmatory-causal and explanatory fashion.

Smyth (1954:638) also considers γάρ glossed as 'in fact, indeed' to be confirmatory adverb and, glossed as 'for', a causal conjunction. According to Smyth (loc. cit.), "γάρ is especially common in sentences which offer a reason for, or an explanation of, a preceding or following statement." He indicates that in many cases it is not clear whether γάρ is a conjunction or an adverb marking assurance.

In sum, γάρ in Classical Greek has a dual orientation: as an adverb, glossed 'in fact, indeed', and as a conjunction, glossed 'for'. All the scholars agree that the conjunctive function of γάρ is primarily causal; some hold that it is also explanatory. The confirmatory connective idea 'for' developed from the adverbial orientation, and the causal and explanatory uses are both related to it.

3.2 How traditional scholars of New Testament Greek view γάρ

The view of Denniston (1954:56-114) mentioned in section 3.1 provides a basis for seeing γάρ as a confirmatory connective in Classical Greek. In New Testament times, too, the confirmatory connective function is present, underlying the manifestation of the causal and explanatory uses of γάρ, although there is no indication that the adverbial γάρ is still in use. (Some may see some intimations of this.) It is my view (see sec. 3.4) that in the New Testament the confirmatory connective function is primary, reason and explanation being particular uses of this function in specific contexts. Traditional scholars of New Testament Greek, however, maintain that the primary function of γάρ is causal, with additional functions of inference, continuation, explanation and resumption.[2]

---

[2] In the New Testament γάρ is one of the most frequently used of the conjunctions. It appears 1,036 times. In Romans alone Paul employs it 143 times. Matthew uses it 124 times. In comparison, John has it rather seldom: 64 times in the Gospel, 6 times in his letters, and 16 times in Revelation (BDR 1976:382). In the pastoral epistles it appears 33 times (macBible 1988).

Γάρ AS A MARKER OF CONFIRMATION   31

BAGD (1979:151-52), for example, present γάρ as a conjunction used to state cause, inference, continuation, and explanation. They state that as an expression of cause/reason γάρ means 'for', as in Rom. 1:9 (witness γάρ mine is God); as an expression of inference, 'certainly, by all means', as in 1 Pet. 4:15 (not γάρ let one suffer as a murderer); as an expression of continuation, 'yes, indeed' as in 1 Thess. 2:20 (you γάρ are our glory); and as an explanation 'for, you see', as in Rom. 7:2 (the γάρ woman is bound by law to her husband while he lives). In a weakened sense they say γάρ is sometimes resumptive, especially in long periodic sentences like Rom. 15:27 (they were pleased γάρ, and they are in debt to them; if γάρ the Gentiles have come to share in their spiritual blessings . . .). While all these different ideas can be understood as different uses, I tend to agree with Larsen (1991:36) who says that BAGD assigns "too many and varied meanings to γάρ."

BDR (1976: 382-83) are in agreement with BAGD's claim that γάρ is one of the most frequently used conjunctions in the New Testament. According to them, its usage is the same as in Classical Greek; that is, it is primarily causal (see Moulton and Turner 1963:331), but also explanatory and often appears in questions as in Matt. 27:23 (what γάρ evil did he do?). Frequently it turns up in answers which stress that which was asked for, as in 1 Cor. 9:10 (because of us γάρ it was written). While the collocation of καί and γάρ can mean 'for', more often these two have no inner connection and are simply a sequence 'for also'.

3.3 How discourse linguists view γάρ in the New Testament

Discourse linguists nearly all conclude that γάρ has one basic function, backwards confirmation (i.e., referring back to a previous proposition). The confirmation may provide strengthening, reason, or explanation.

Blass (1993:5-6) approaches the function of γάρ from a relevance theory perspective. She sees it as marking "propositions designed to support the conclusion." Thus γάρ does two things: it not only marks a proposition as a premise but a premise that "backwards confirms," and thereby strengthens, a conclusion. For example, in Rom. 3:22b-23a (not γάρ is there a difference), 'there is no difference' strengthens the last part of the previous proposition, 'the righteousness of God through faith in Jesus Christ (is) for all who believe'.

Blass notes further that γάρ can mark new as well as known information. When information is known, it does not have to be the information stated in the previous proposition but can be an assumption available to the hearer/reader. In a case like this, the proposition introduced by γάρ is strengthening an assumption. For example, in Rom. 5:7 (hardly γάρ will someone die for a righteous person), it is not the previous proposition (for Christ . . . died for the ungodly) which is strengthened, but an assumption attributed to the readers: (people do not die for the ungodly). This in turn strengthens the assertion of v. 5 (reiterated in v. 8) that Christ's death graphically illustrates the love of God.

Levinsohn (1992:58) writes regarding γάρ, "Parenthetical comments that do not involve fronting are usually introduced with δέ or γάρ." Earlier he said,

"When δέ introduces a background[3] comment about the previous sentence, it is not intended to explain anything" (Levinsohn 1980:266). In contrast, γάρ, he says, introduces an explanation or exposition of the previous assertion (p. 59).

According to Poythress (1984:319–20), γάρ introduces vague logical support for what precedes. In his terms for propositional relations this means that "γάρ indicates a relationship of implication-grounds or result-reason." Thus he appears to perceive the function of γάρ as supportive.

According to Larsen (1991b:36–38), γάρ is an explanatory particle that introduces further information for better understanding of a word or an aspect of a previous clause or sentence and, though it is an explanatory particle, it can function causally in an appropriate context. In narrative texts it usually introduces background information as in Mark 16:4 (the stone was rolled away, γάρ it was great). In non-narrative texts it provides further explanation/comment on an aspect of a previous sentence. An example of this is in Rom. 1:15–16: γάρ the gospel is the power of God. Paul uses γάρ quite extensively, especially in his argumentative sections such as Rom. 1:15–20.

In sum, while traditional New Testament scholars claim that γάρ expresses a number of functions from reason to resumption, with reason, however, predominating, discourse linguists narrow its function to that of a background marker, providing confirmation or support for a previous proposition or assumption. Some describe it as an explanatory or expository particle that introduces further information for a better understanding of a word or an aspect of a previous proposition; this is still confirmation or support. Others hold that it introduces a *reason* in support of the previous proposition or assumption. In any case, the specific uses are determined by the context. In the following section I will demonstrate on the basis of the pastoral epistles data that the basic function of conjunctive γάρ is indeed confirmatory and that reason and explanation are particular uses in specific contexts.

3.4 The use of γάρ in the pastoral Epistles

Although scholars of Classical Greek considered γάρ to be primarily a causal conjunction, γάρ rarely marks cause, in the strict sense of the word, in the pastoral epistles. More often it gives a *reason* for a previous assertion; that is, it introduces a clause that "explains the occurrence or nature of an effect" (*The American Heritage Dictionary* 1982:214 [see *cause*]).

The one passage in which the proposition introduced by γάρ comes closest to describing the *cause* of the previous assertion is 1 Timothy 4:5, *cause* being defined as that which "must exist for an effect logically to occur" (loc. cit.).

1 Tim. 4:4 ὅτι   πᾶν   κτίσμα   θεοῦ   καλόν, καὶ   οὐδὲν   ἀπόβλητον
         that   all   creation of-God good   and   nothing to-be-rejected

---

[3] I assume that "parenthetical comment" and "background comment" mean the same thing in this context (see Levinsohn 1992:59).

μετὰ εὐχαριστίας λαμβανόμενον
with thanksgiving being-received

'For everything created by God is good, and nothing is to be rejected if it is received with thanksgiving;'

5 ἁγιάζεται **γὰρ** διὰ λόγου θεοῦ καὶ ἐντεύξεως.
it-is-sanctified γάρ through word of-God and prayer

'for then it is consecrated by the word of God and prayer.'

In the preceding passage Paul counters false piety by pointing out that nothing of God's creation needs to be rejected when received with thanksgiving. Here one can nearly understand the function of γάρ in a causal sense in that what has been 'consecrated by the word of God and prayer' is good. But even so, v. 5 should probably be viewed only as the reason for Paul's conviction.

The next examples illustrate propositions introduced by γάρ that are clearly the reason for a previous clause, sentence, or paragraph:

1 Tim. 4:7a τοὺς δὲ βεβήλους καὶ γραώδεις μύθους παραιτοῦ.
the but profane and old-womanish myths decline

'Have nothing to do with godless and silly myths.'

7b γύμναζε δὲ σεαυτὸν πρὸς εὐσέβειαν·
exercise but yourself toward godliness

'Train yourself in godliness;'

8 ἡ **γὰρ** σωματικὴ γυμνασία πρὸς ὀλίγον ἐστὶν ὠφέλιμος,
the γάρ bodily exercise for little is useful

ἡ δὲ εὐσέβεια πρὸς πάντα ὠφέλιμός ἐστιν,
the but godliness for all useful is

ἐπαγγελίαν ἔχουσα ζωῆς τῆς νῦν καὶ τῆς μελλούσης
promise having of-life the now and the coming

'for while bodily training is of some value, godliness is of value in every way, as it holds the promise for the present life and also for the life to come.'

In 1 Tim. 4:7b Paul directs Timothy: γύμναζε δὲ σεαυτὸν πρὸς εὐσέβειαν 'exercise yourself in respect to godliness'. Then follows the reason for his injunction introduced by γάρ in v. 8. Knight (1992:197) writes, "γάρ joins this verse [v. 8] to v. 7b and provides the grounds (i.e., reason) for the exhortation of v. 7b."

Another example is in 1 Tim. 2:3–6:

1 Tim. 2:3 τοῦτο καλὸν καὶ ἀπόδεκτον ἐνώπιον τοῦ σωτῆρος ἡμῶν θεοῦ,
this good and acceptable before the savior of-us God

'This is good, and is acceptable in the sight of God our Savior,'

4 ὃς πάντας ἀνθρώπους θέλει σωθῆναι
   who all   people   wants to-attain-salvation

καὶ εἰς ἐπίγνωσιν ἀληθείας ἐλθεῖν.
and into knowledge of-truth to-come

'who desires all men to be saved and to come to the knowledge of the truth.'

5 εἷς **γὰρ** θεός, εἷς καὶ μεσίτης θεοῦ
   one **γάρ** God   one also mediator of-God

καὶ ἀνθρώπων, ἄνθρωπος Χριστὸς Ἰησοῦς,
and people man Christ Jesus

'For there is one God, and there is one mediator between God and men, the man Christ Jesus,'

6 ὁ δοὺς ἑαυτὸν ἀντίλυτρον ὑπὲρ πάντων,
  who giving himself payment on-behalf-of all

τὸ μαρτύριον καιροῖς ἰδίοις
the testimony at-times own

'who gave himself as a ransom for all, the testimony to which was borne at the proper time.'

In 1 Tim. 2:4 Paul indicates that God 'wants all people to attain salvation', πάντας ἀνθρώπους θέλει σωθῆναι, not as a wish but as a goal. Conjunctive γάρ in v. 5 introduces the oneness of God and his redemptive purpose through his Son as the reason for his desire that all people attain salvation. In support of this, I cite Graham: "The apostle wishes by it [γάρ] to confirm the idea of the universality of the divine purpose of salvation as true and necessary: he does this first by pointing to the unity of God ... From the unity of God, it necessarily follows that there is only one purpose regarding all ..." (1976:83–84).

Titus 2:9 δούλους ἰδίοις δεσπόταις ὑποτάσσεσθαι
          slaves to-own masters to-submit

ἐν πᾶσιν, εὐαρέστους εἶναι,
in all pleasing to-be

'Bid slaves to be submissive to their masters and to give satisfaction in every respect;'

10a μὴ ἀντιλέγοντας μὴ νοσφιζομένους,
     not speaking-against not stealing

ἀλλὰ πᾶσαν πίστιν ἐνδεικνυμένους ἀγαθήν,
but all faith showing good

'they are not to be refractory, nor to pilfer, but to show entire and true fidelity,'

10b ἵνα   τὴν διδασκαλίαν τὴν τοῦ   σωτῆρος
    so-that   the teaching   the of-the savior

    ἡμῶν   θεοῦ κοσμῶσιν   ἐν πᾶσιν
    of-us God they-do-credit-to in all

    'so that in everything they may adorn the doctrine of God our Savior.'

11 Ἐπεφάνη **γὰρ** ἡ χάρις τοῦ θεοῦ σωτήριος πᾶσιν ἀνθρώποις,
   appeared γάρ   the grace of-the God saving   for-all people

   'For the grace of God has appeared for the salvation of all men,'

12 παιδεύουσα ἡμᾶς ἵνα   ἀρνησάμενοι τὴν ἀσέβειαν
   teaching   us   that denying   the godlessness

   καὶ τὰς κοσμικὰς ἐπιθυμίας σωφρόνως καὶ δικαίως
   and the worldly desires   soberly   and righteously

   καὶ εὐσεβῶς ζήσωμεν   ἐν τῷ νῦν αἰῶνι,
   and godly   we-may-live in the now age

   'training us to renounce irreligion and worldly passions, and to live sober, upright, and godly lives in this world.'

In Titus 2:9–10a Paul urges slaves to show faithfulness to their masters in all things. The reason for such action is in v. 11, introduced with γάρ: the grace of God which comes through teaching and motivates people to godly living (see BAGD 1979:377).

There are a few passages in which the proposition introduced by γάρ gives a reason not for the previous assertion itself, but for something which follows from it. In 1 Tim. 3:12 is an example of such passages:

1 Tim. 3:12 διάκονοι ἔστωσαν μιᾶς   γυναικὸς ἄνδρες,
            deacons let-be   of-one wife   husbands

    τέκνων   καλῶς προϊστάμενοι καὶ τῶν ἰδίων οἴκων·
    children well managing   and the own   household

    'Let deacons be the husband of one wife, and let them manage their children and their households well;'

13 οἱ **γὰρ** καλῶς διακονήσαντες βαθμὸν ἑαυτοῖς
   the γάρ   well managing   step   for-themselves

   καλὸν περιποιοῦνται καὶ πολλὴν παρρησίαν
   good make   and much   boldness

   ἐν πίστει τῇ ἐν Χριστῷ Ἰησοῦ.
   in faith the in Christ Jesus

   'for those who serve well as deacons gain a good stand for themselves and also great confidence in the faith which is in Christ Jesus.'

It should be noted that 1 Tim. 3:8-12 say nothing about serving as deacons; rather, they describe the character and circumstances of deacons; the conjunctive γάρ therefore introduces a reason not for the exhortation of v. 12, but for an implied proposition like 'such people will serve well as deacons'.

Occasionally even "reason" seems too strong a word to describe the function of the proposition introduced by γάρ, as in 1 Tim. 4.

1 Tim. 4:8b ἡ   δὲ   εὐσέβεια   πρὸς   πάντα   ὠφέλιμός   ἐστιν,
          the   but godliness   for   all   useful   is

ἐπαγγελίαν   ἔχουσα   ζωῆς   τῆς   νῦν   καὶ   τῆς   μελλούσης
promise   having   of-life   the   now   and   the   coming

'godliness is of value in every way, as it holds the promise for the present life and also for the life to come.'

9 πιστὸς   ὁ   λόγος   καὶ   πάσης   ἀποδοχῆς   ἄξιος·
  faithful   the   word   and   of-all   acceptance worthy

'The saying is sure and worthy of full acceptance.'

10 εἰς τοῦτο[4] γὰρ   κοπιῶμεν   καὶ   ἀγωνιζόμεθα,
   for this   γάρ   we-struggle   and   toil

ὅτι   ἠλπίκαμεν   ἐπὶ   θεῷ   ζῶντι,
because   we-have-hoped   upon   God   living,

ὅς   ἐστιν   σωτὴρ   πάντων   ἀνθρώπων,   μάλιστα   πιστῶν.
who   is   savior of-all   people   especially of-believers

'For to this end we toil and strive, because we have our hope set on the living God, who is the Savior of all men, especially of those who believe.'

If we assume that v. 9 refers back to 8b (Knight 1992:201 calls it a citation-commendation formula referring to what precedes), then v. 10, introduced by γάρ, can be said to confirm and strengthen the fact that the word (that godliness is useful for everything) is faithful and worthy of full acceptance. The fact of our toiling and striving "to this end" is evidence for the sureness of the saying. But to see this as a reason is problematic because εἰς τοῦτο itself means 'for this reason'.

3.5 Conclusion

Blass's description of γάρ as a signal of strengthening/confirmation seems the best way to describe its function, since it readily covers the majority of its occurrences, both those in which it involves a "reason" and those which tend towards cause (e.g., 1 Tim. 4:5), and even those in which even reason seems to be a term that does not quite apply (e.g., 1 Tim. 4:10).

---

[4] BAGD (1979:229) translate this 'for this reason or purpose' (see Rom. 14:9, 2 Cor. 2:9).

4 Δέ As a Marker of Development

There are two major views on δέ: Traditional linguists ascribe two functions to it, adversative and copulative; discourse linguists, one, it has something to do with change, variously described as "change of context," "significant change," "next step," or "development." While to say δέ has a single function is a step in the right direction, the concept of change creates its own problems, viz. what the significance of change is, how change activated by δέ is different from that initiated by ἀλλά 'but', and how the clause introduced by δέ relates to the previous conjunct.

Levinsohn's view is that δέ marks development of the argument. He clarifies what the significance of change is, how the function of δέ is different from ἀλλά, and how the proposition introduced by δέ relates to what precedes and follows. He does, however, face one obstacle, as will be seen (sec. 4.4.3), and that is the matter of the parenthetical use of δέ.

Each occurrence of δέ in the pastoral epistles except one supports the view that δέ is a developmental marker. In my view, even the parenthetical use of δέ can be viewed as developmental to a degree. There are also special constructions, such as οὐ μόνον δέ ... ἀλλὰ καί, the correlation μέν ... δέ, and the collocation of δέ with καί, in which δέ maintains its developmental function. All of these will be discussed in this chapter.

The traditional view of δέ is that it is an adversative and copulative marker, stronger than καί and weaker than ἀλλά. This was the dominant persuasion of scholars for a long time, though they intimate that the thought of adversative was primary. It was not until the midseventies that the insights of descriptive linguistics began to be applied to conjunctions in the New Testament. Levinsohn (1977) was one of the earliest discourse scholars who studied this area and came up with some stimulating results. Discourse linguists generally hold that δέ has one basic function, namely as a marker of change.

4.1 How traditional scholars of Classical Greek view δέ

Liddell and Scott (1940:371) translate the particle δέ as 'but'. They describe it as an adversative, expressing contrast, opposition, or antithesis (Barnhart and Stein 1958:18) and as a copulative particle commonly corresponding to μέν, which may often be rendered 'while, whereas, on the other hand' (in Thucydides 1.12). When μέν is omitted, according to Liddell and Scott (loc. cit.), which happens frequently, δέ is used in an adversative fashion, "expressing distinct opposition" (in Homer's *Iliad* 1.108). It appears in questions which imply opposition (in Xenophon's *Cyrus* 5.1.4). Its presence implies causal connection, though less direct than γάρ (in Homer's *Iliad* 6.160). It also performs copulative functions. This function is seen in explanatory clauses (in Thucydides 4.66),[1] in enumerations or transitions (Xenophon's *Cyrus* 1.2.1), and in answering to τε (Plato's *Republic* 367C). Together with τί it marks a transition in dialogue and can be translated 'what then'. It is used in apodoses after hypothetical clauses, where it is translated 'then' (Homer's *Iliad* 1.137), and after temporal or relative clauses (Herodotus 9.70). When used to resume a discourse after an interruption or parenthesis, it may be translated 'I say, now, so then' (Herodotus 1.28, 29). It is also used to begin a story after a pause (Homer's *Odyssey* 4.400). And finally, it can be employed to introduce a proof.

Smyth (1956:644) summarizes well the main point Liddell and Scott want to make:

> δέ serves to mark that something is different from what precedes, but only to offset it, not to exclude or contradict it; it denotes only a slight contrast, and is therefore weaker than ἀλλά, but stronger than καί. Δέ is adversative and copulative; but the two uses are not always clearly to be distinguished.

Although Liddell and Scott and Smyth appear to identify two distinct functions for δέ, copulative and adversative (i.e., contrastive), Smyth does here intimate that δέ has a single basic function. As he says, the major impact of δέ is to mark something as different in order to set it off from something else.

4.2 How traditional scholars of New Testament Greek view δέ

New Testament scholars likewise identify two functions of δέ,[2] contrastive and copulative. Of its use, BAGD (1979:171) say that it is

> used to connect one clause with another when it is felt that there is some contrast between them, though the contrast is often scarcely discernible. The most common translations of δέ are: *but*, when a contrast is clearly implied; *and*, when a simple connective is desired, without contrast; frequently it cannot be translated at all.

The following illustrates their claims:

(a) *Re the contrastive function of* δέ

> When δέ functions contrastively, it brings out contrast in general, as in 1 Cor. 2:14-15:
>
> > The nonspiritual person does not have the things of the Spirit of God, he is unable to know [them], because they are spiritually discerned.

---

[1] In the 1897 edition Liddell and Scott state, "δέ sometimes subjoins a clause in such a manner as to denote connexion of cause and effect, when it might be replaced by γάρ" (p. 327). However, Winer (1877:566-67) argues that δέ never means 'for'. See also the discussion on 1 Tim. 3:4-5 in section 4.4.3.

[2] BAGD (1979:171) write that δέ is one of the most common Greek particles, being the second most frequently used conjunction in the New Testament, appearing 2771 times (BDR 1976:377), 59 times in the pastoral epistles alone (acCordance 1994).

> The δέ spiritual person discerns all things, he δέ himself is discerned by no one.

After a negative δέ can be translated 'rather', as in Rom. 3:4:

> by no means. Let δέ God be true.

It can also contrast an apodosis with the protasis, as in Col. 1:21-22:

> ... enemies in reference to the mind because of evil works,
> now δέ he reconciled by the body of his flesh through his death.

When the resumptive sentence contrasts with the proposition prior to the interruption, δέ marks the resumption of an interrupted discourse, as in Rom. 5:6-8:

> For while we were yet weak, Christ still died on behalf of godless people at the right time. For someone will hardly die on behalf of a righteous person.
> For on behalf of a good person someone perhaps dares to die.
> God commends δέ his love toward us that while we were yet sinners Christ died on behalf of us.

(b) *Re the copulative function of* δέ

As a plain connective, δέ very frequently acts as "a transitional particle pure and simple, without any contrast intended *now, then*" (BAGD 1979:171), as in Rom. 8:27-28:

> ... because according to God's will he [the Spirit] intercedes for the saints. We know δέ that for those who love God all things work for good ...

In a list of similar things δέ brings out a clearer separation, as in 2 Pet. 1:5b-7:

> supply your faith with virtue, δέ virtue with knowledge,
> δέ knowledge with self-control, δέ self-control with endurance. . . .

It also relates one teaching to another, as in Rom. 13:14b-4:1a:

> Do not make any provisions for the flesh to obtain its desires.
> The δέ weak person in faith receive.

That δέ is a plain connective becomes especially apparent when it is used to insert an explanation. In this case it may be translated 'that is', as in Rom. 3:21-22:

> But now apart from the law the righteousness of God is revealed . . .
> the righteousness δέ of God through faith in Jesus Christ.

I consider it an overstatement that, as BAGD claim "frequently it [δέ] cannot be translated at all." What Titrud (1991:5) says regarding καί is also true of δέ, "There is a pragmatic difference between the use of καί and its nonuse, even though it may be slight." I hold that δέ always signals a constraint on the two constituents which it conjoins (see Blass 1993:14).

In sum, traditional scholars both of Classical Greek and the New Testament indicate that δέ has a dual function, adversative (i.e., contrastive) and copulative (i.e., connective or transitional). At the same time they note that the basic function of δέ is contrast, "to connect one clause with another when it is felt that there is some contrast between them" (BAGD 1979:171). Perhaps Smyth (1954:644) is even more to the point: "to mark that something is different from what precedes" (though the contrast or difference is at times hardly discernible). This leads me to conclude that for these scholars the basic function of δέ is to mark something as different. Only when the difference is not discernible is it taken to function in a copulative fashion.

4.3 How discourse linguists view δέ in the New Testament

Discourse linguists, while they may employ different terms for it, hold that δέ has only one basic function. This is in agreement with the intimation expressed by traditional linguists. The different uses can be related to that one basic function.

Buth (1991, 1992) says that δέ is a "signal that something has changed," that it is used to mark a "significant change" that has occurred. This is the basic function of δέ. He states further, however, that δέ has a number of different uses in the Gospel of John:

1. It presents "background information," such as descriptions and interrupting comments (John 6:70–71).
2. It introduces "switch subject" with pronoun/article, ὁ δέ or οἱ δέ, to refer to a different subject from the one in the previous sentence or clause (John 2:8).
3. It marks "contrast" with the preceding context (John 11:45–46).
4. It highlights a new unit or an event complex (John 11:54–55).
5. It spotlights on-line and significant change[3] (John 12:3).

All of these uses have one thing in common: in one way or another they all indicate change.

Kathleen Callow (1992), working with 1 Corinthians, views the function of δέ similarly: "The speaker uses δέ as a signal, saying, 'This is the next step.' It may be a little step or a big one, it may be a step forward, or sideways, or even backward-looking, but it is always the next step, and with it the speaker or writer is progressing one thought at a time along a purposeful line of development" (pp. 191–92). As far as she is concerned, all uses of a particle have "some shared factor of meaning at a very generalized level" (p. 184).

---

[3] Buth (1991, 1992) compares "on-line and significant change" to Levinsohn's "development." He was writing in response to a 1989 lecture by Levinsohn, as well as Levinsohn's 1981 article (Levinsohn p.c.).

This "shared factor of meaning" can be arrived at through studying "multiple functions." She proceeds to note (1992:184–87) that the span (i.e., level) in which the conjunction appears helps identify its function. She identifies the functions of δέ according to its use in a "long span," a "short span," and an "intermediate span":

The long span function of δέ:
1. It signals major change from the preceding material (1 Cor. 7:25).
2. It terminates discussion of a topic signaled by a generic term with back-reference (1 Cor. 9:23).

The short span function of δέ:
1. It signals contrast with obvious contrasting elements (1 Cor. 13:12)
2. It marks an aside—an exception or restriction—or, with different signals, an explanation (1 Cor. 10:4a).
3. It marks a listing, sometimes with cumulative and climactic effect (1 Cor. 3:23).

The intermediate span function of δέ:
1. It introduces a new aspect of an existing topic (1 Cor. 4:18).
2. After a topic is introduced, successive points are marked by δέ, while supporting material is presented with γάρ, ὁμοίως, particles, etc. (1 Cor. 10:7–10).
3. At times in an intermediate span δέ functions as in a short span (1 Cor. 4:18–19).

But whatever the different uses of δέ may be in a particular context, the basic function is always to indicate the next step which the author takes in his presentation.[4]

Levinsohn (1992:32) claims that δέ is a developmental conjunction: "δέ typically is found when the information it introduces develops from what has preceded it...." In expository text, he explains, "it is a development marker, in the sense that the information it introduces builds on what has gone before and makes a distinct contribution to the argument..." (p. 64). The two key points are: 'builds on what has gone before' and 'makes a distinct contribution to the argument'.

Levinsohn (p. 31) says that δέ also introduces "parenthetical comments." But he is not suggesting two functions of δέ, a developmental one and one that introduces parenthetical comments, as he hastens to say: "More accurately, δέ is a developmental-antidevelopmental conjunction, since it also introduces paren-

---

[4] Callow (1992:192) has also detected the presence of emotion as a motivating factor for the presence or absence of δέ in 1 Corinthians. When the development is logical and linear, δέ is present; when the message is emotional or dwells on a point, it is absent. This cannot be verified for the pastoral epistles since the texts do not involve such emotion.

thetical comments' (p. 31, fn. 1). He holds that δέ has one basic function, the developmental one, which somehow includes parenthetical comments.

In Blass's view (1993), δέ places a constraint on the relevance of the utterance or statement it introduces (p. 13). "The constraint function ... instructs the hearer to change the major context against which the speaker intends the hearer to process the new information" (p. 17). She concludes, "As a matter of fact in each case the hearer is alerted to abandon an available context" (p. 18). According to Blass, then, δέ has one basic function, namely, to instruct the hearer "to abandon an available context." She identifies three different contexts in which δέ is used.

1. Denial of expectation (Rom. 8:8–9):

   Those ... who are in the flesh are unable to please God.
   We δέ are not in the flesh but [ἀλλά] in the Spirit.

2. Contrast (Rom. 8:5):

   for those who are fleshly think the things of the flesh;
   those δέ who are spiritual, the things of the Spirit.

3. Main context change, that is, moving from one context to another (Rom. 8:7b–8):

   for he does not submit to the law of God, for he is not able.
   Those δέ who are in the flesh are unable to please God.

But notice the similarity in all three instances: the hearer is called to change from an available context to a new context which corrects a wrong expectation, negates the first conjunct, or changes the main context.

As mentioned earlier, traditional linguists also point to δέ as having one basic function, though they admitted that at times it functioned in a copulative fashion and came up with two glosses for δέ: 'but' when the difference between the clauses connected by it was evident, and 'and' when it was not. The main difference between *their* view and that of the discourse linguists is the latter's awareness of the many *uses* of the single-function δέ, one of them being copulative. (The discourse linguists all see the basic function of δέ to be as a marker of change, development.) Of course, among the discourse linguists themselves there are differences in the way they understand δέ's single function. For example, some think of "development" as one of the uses of δέ (Buth, Blass); Levinsohn, on the other hand, lists "contrast," "listing," "switch reference," "new unit," etc., all as instances of the development function. In the next section I will show that the pastoral epistles bear out Levinsohn's understanding of δέ as a marker of development.

4.4 The use of δέ in the pastoral Epistles

In section 4.4.1 I will present those texts in the pastoral epistles in which δέ is considered a copulative, that is, with δέ leading from one proposition to the next. In section 4.4.2 I will present those texts in which the use of δέ is generally considered to be contrastive. My goal is to show that δέ is developmental whether its use is copulative or contrastive.

4.4.1 Δέ as copulative

In the following passages I consider the δέ to be copulative. My purpose here is to demonstrate that, in each of these passages, the function of the copulative δέ is developmental. (In section 4.4.2 the contrastive δέ will likewise be shown to be developmental in function.)

2 Tim. 1:5a ὑπόμνησιν λαβὼν τῆς ἐν σοὶ ἀνυποκρίτου πίστεως,
remembrance having-taken of-the in you genuine faith
'I am reminded of your sincere faith,'

5b ἥτις ἐνῴκησεν πρῶτον ἐν τῇ μάμμῃ σου Λωΐδι
which dwelled first in the grandmother of-you Lois

καὶ τῇ μητρί σου Εὐνίκῃ,
and the mother of-you Eunice

'a faith that dwelt first in your grandmother Lois and your mother Eunice'

5c πέπεισμαι **δὲ** ὅτι καὶ ἐν σοί.
I-am-convinced **δέ** that also in you

'and now, I am sure, dwells in you.'

Knight (1992:368) states, "Paul adds for emphasis and as an encouragement to Timothy πέπεισμαι δὲ ὅτι ἐν σοί." Minor (1992:14) takes this δέ as copulative, translating it 'and'. acCordance (1994) classifies it as continuative. Another support for seeing δέ as copulative is the adverbial καί in 5c, which associates ἐν σοί 'in you (Timothy)' with ἐν τῇ μάμμῃ σου Λωΐδι καὶ τῇ μητρί σου Εὐνίκῃ 'in your grandmother Lois and your mother Eunice'. Thus δέ is to be taken as copulative in this text rather than contrastive.

The question is whether δέ marks development. I conclude that it does, for two reasons: The clause which δέ introduces builds on what precedes, the faith of the grandmother and mother of Timothy, which was discussed in 5a. And it adds information that advances Paul's argument, namely that Timothy has faith (see Knight 1992:369).

1 Tim. 1:3 Καθὼς παρεκάλεσά σε προσμεῖναι ἐν Ἐφέσῳ
just-as I-commanded you to-stay in Ephesus

πορευόμενος εἰς Μακεδονίαν,
going into Macedonia

ἵνα παραγγείλῃς τισὶν μὴ ἑτεροδιδασκαλεῖν
so-that you-might-instruct some not to-teach-different-doctrine

'As I urged you when I was going to Macedonia, remain at Ephesus that you may charge certain persons not to teach a different doctrine,'

4 μηδὲ προσέχειν   μύθοις καὶ γενεαλογίαις ἀπεράντοις,
  nor to-pay-attention-to myths and genealogies endless

αἵτινες ἐκζητήσεις παρέχουσιν
which   arguments   bring-about

μᾶλλον ἢ οἰκονομίαν θεοῦ   τὴν ἐν πίστει·
rather than training   from-God the in faith

'nor to occupy themselves with myths and endless genealogies which promote speculations rather than the divine training that is in faith;'

5 τὸ **δὲ** τέλος τῆς παραγγελίας ἐστὶν ἀγάπη
  the **δέ** purpose of-the instruction is love

ἐκ   καθαρᾶς καρδίας καὶ συνειδήσεως ἀγαθῆς
from pure   heart   and conscience good

καὶ πίστεως ἀνυποκρίτου
and faith   genuine

'whereas the aim of our charge is love that issues from a pure heart and a good conscience and sincere faith.'

Knight (1992:76) claims that in 1 Tim. 1:5 δέ points up a *contrast* between "the heterodox way (v. 4) and the apostolic way (v. 5)." This cannot be right, since the thrust of v. 3 is that Timothy is instructing certain ones not to teach false doctrine. What in v. 5 is the purpose for the instruction? Here δέ is classified by acCordance (1994) as "continuative" (i.e., copulative). In fact, the majority of commentators (those cited by Graham 1976:19) also take it to be copulative.

As in 2 Tim. 1:5, the δέ in 1 Tim. 1:5 introduces a clause of development. There are two reasons for concluding this: The initial reference in v. 5 to τῆς παραγγελίας 'the instruction' builds on παραγγείλῃς 'you may instruct' in v. 3. Also v. 5 makes a significant contribution to the topic of instruction with the new point of departure[5] τὸ ... τέλος (the purpose or goal [of instruction]), which Paul then describes.

2 Tim. 2:19 ὁ   μέντοι   στερεὸς θεμέλιος τοῦ   θεοῦ ἕστηκεν,
            the nevertheless firm   foundation of-the God stands

ἔχων   τὴν σφραγίδα ταύτην ἔγνω κύριος τοὺς ὄντας αὐτοῦ,
having the seal   this   knows Lord   the being his

---

[5] "A point of departure is a fronted constituent placed at the beginning of a clause or sentence both to set a 'domain' for what follows ... and to provide the primary basis for relating what follows to the context" (Levinsohn 1992:18). (A fronted constituent is any constituent placed before the verb.)

καί, ἀποστήτω ἀπὸ ἀδικίας πᾶς
and let-abstain from wickedness everyone

ὁ ὀνομάζων τὸ ὄνομα κυρίου
the calls-on the name of-Lord

'But God's firm foundation stands, bearing this seal: "The Lord knows those who are his," and, "Let every one who names the name of the Lord depart from iniquity".'

20 Ἐν μεγάλῃ **δὲ** οἰκίᾳ οὐκ ἔστιν μόνον σκεύη
in great <u>δέ</u> house not is only vessels

χρυσᾶ καὶ ἀργυρᾶ ἀλλὰ καὶ ξύλινα καὶ ὀστράκινα,
golden and silver but also wood and clay

καὶ ἃ μὲν εἰς τιμὴν ἃ δὲ εἰς ἀτιμίαν
and what on-the- into honor what but into dishonor
one-hand

'In a great house there are not only vessels of gold and silver but also of wood and earthenware, and some for noble use, some for ignoble.'

In v. 20 δέ is copulative. This is supported by Knight (1992:417) who translates it 'now', and calls it a transitional particle; acCordance (1994) categorizes it under "continuative"; Lock (1924:101) calls it an illustration. Even though the majority of the authorities (those cited by Minor 1992:79) take δέ as contrastive, nevertheless the common thread between v. 19 and v. 20 shows that δέ is transitional, not contrastive: Verse 19 speaks of 'God's firm foundation' and v. 20 of a 'noble household'. And not only does θεμέλιος 'foundation' correspond with οἰκίᾳ 'house', but ἀδικίας 'wickedness' corresponds with ἀτιμίαν 'dishonor'.

Clearly δέ is a marker of development in this passage since vv. 20-21 build on v. 19. There is a section here made up of vv. 19-21 in which the first point (in v. 19) is "reassurance to Timothy" (Lock 1924:100). Moffat summarizes the content of these verses in these words as "the true and optimistic conception of the Church in relation to all teachers, true and false" (cited by Travis 1972:4).

The section (vv.19-21) is introduced by ὁ ... στερεὸς θεμέλιος 'the firm foundation', a point of departure, which is conjoined with μέντοι 'nevertheless', an adversative particle separating vv. 19-21 from the preceding verses. The second point of this section is marked with a new point of departure, in v. 20, showing that it builds on what precedes.

The new point of departure is ἐν μεγάλῃ ... οἰκίᾳ 'in a great house' which is collocated with δέ. Although a number of commentators consider vv. 20-21 as a separate section (Travis 1972:106), they make a distinct contribution to the line of argument started in v. 19. This is clear from the text which not only begins with a new point of departure but goes on to show that God's people will be vessels for honor (εἰς τίμην), whenever they cleanse themselves from the things (ἀπὸ τούτων) which false teachers induce them to do (in v. 21).

The following passage is yet another one in which the copulative δέ is used to mark development:

1 Tim. 3:16 καὶ ὁμολογουμένως μέγα ἐστὶν τὸ τῆς εὐσεβείας μυστήριον·
and indeed great is the of-the godliness mystery

Ὃ ἐφανερώθη ἐν σαρκί, ἐδικαιώθη ἐν πνεύματι,
who was-manifested in flesh justified in Spirit

ὤφθη ἀγγέλοις, ἐκηρύχθη ἐν ἔθνεσιν,
appeared-to angels proclaimed among Gentiles

ἐπιστεύθη ἐν κόσμῳ, ἀνελήμφθη ἐν δόξῃ.
believed in world taken-up in glory

'Great indeed, we confess, is the mystery of our religion:
He was manifested in the flesh, vindicated in the Spirit,
seen by angels, preached among the nations,
believed on in the world, taken up in glory.'

4:1 Τὸ **δὲ** πνεῦμα ῥητῶς λέγει ὅτι ἐν ὑστέροις καιροῖς
the **δέ** spirit plainly says that in latter times

ἀποστήσονταί τινες τῆς πίστεως, προσέχοντες
will-fall-away some from-the faith paying-attention

πνεύμασιν πλάνοις καὶ διδασκαλίαις δαιμονίων
to-spirits deceptive and teachings of-demons

'Now the Spirit expressly says that in later times some will depart from the faith by giving heed to deceitful spirits and doctrines of demons.'

The majority of the authorities cited by Graham (1976:190–91) take δέ in 1 Tim. 4:1 to be contrastive. There is another large group which does not comment on it at all. A minority take it to be copulative. In acCordance (1994), for example, it is classified as "continuative." I follow acCordance and take it to be copulative. It is possible to make a good point for this conclusion in light of there being a new point of departure (τὸ ... πνεῦμα ... λέγει) in 4:1 (see 1 Tim. 3:14 ταῦτα γράφω).

The reasons for ascribing to δέ a developmental function are two: First, 4:1 makes reference to τῆς πίστεως 'the faith', building on τῆς ἀληθείας 'the truth' (in 3:15) and τὸ τῆς εὐσεβείας μυστήριον 'the mystery of godliness' (in 3:16). Second, δέ introduces 4:1, at the same time contributing to the argument of the preceding verse by describing how people will fall away from the faith.

In each of the four illustrative passages considered in this section we have seen that δέ is more than copulative, it is above all developmental. In other words, the conjunct that it introduces builds on what precedes and makes a distinct contribution to the argument. Thus δέ carries the argument forward. That is its function, just as we saw that the function of ἀλλά is to contrast, and the function of γάρ is to confirm. I want to emphasize again that whether δέ is used in a copulative fashion or not is incidental. What is central is that it functions as a marker of development.

4.4.2 The use of δέ to mark contrast

When we look at the evidence, it is clear that δέ most often occurs in connection with contrast.[6] Out of 59 occurrences of δέ in the pastoral epistles, 38 are contrastive (acCordance 1994). Nevertheless, even in the context of contrast, I would argue that the major function of δέ is development; for when δέ introduces a proposition that contrasts with the previous proposition, it also builds on the previous proposition. In fact, the contrastive δέ always marks development from less relevant to more relevant material.

1 Tim. 4:7b Γύμναζ δὲ σεαυτὸν πρὸς εὐσέβειαν
           train   but yourself for   godliness
          'Train yourself in godliness;'

8a ἡ γὰρ σωματικὴ γυμνασία πρὸς ὀλίγο ἐστὶν ὠφέλιμος,
   the for bodily   exercise for   little is   useful
   'for while bodily training is of some value,'

8b ἡ **δὲ** εὐσέβεια πρὸς πάντα ὠφέλιμός ἐστιν,
   the <u>δέ</u> godliness for   all   useful   is

ἐπαγγελίαν ἔχουσα ζωῆς τῆς νῦν καὶ τῆς μελλούσης.
promise   having of-life the now and the coming

'godliness is of value in every way, as it holds promise for the present life and also for the life to come.'

In 1 Tim. 8b δέ introduces ἡ . . . εὐσέβεια πρὸς πάντα ὠφέλιμός ἐστιν 'godliness is useful in everything' which is a double contrast to ἡ . . . σωματικὴ· γυμνασία πρὸς ὀλίγον ἐστὶν ὠφέλιμος 'physical exercise is of little use'. Knight (1992:199) affirms that δέ in this context is contrastive.

But development is present here as well. My reasoning is as follows: Verse 8, introduced by γάρ, is an explanation of 7b, which says Γύμναζε δὲ σεαυτὸν πρὸς εὐσέβειαν 'but train yourself with regard to godliness'. But 8a does not address the issue of godliness; it simply provides a foil,[7] a constituent of contrast, for 8b. It is 8b that builds on 8a as it addresses the issue. The conjunction δέ that introduces 8b returns to εὐσέβεια 'godliness' (the same word is in 7b) as the new point of departure, contributing to the argument about godliness.

---

[6] "Two items are in contrast when they are 1) perceived as being the same in many respects, 2) perceived as different in few respects, and 3) compared with respect to one or more of these differences" (Mann and Thompson 1987:8).

[7] "A 'foil' is a constituent that is presented for the purpose of being contrasted or added to in the following material. The foil comes into temporary focus in anticipation of a switch of attention to the corresponding constituent" (Levinsohn 1992:84).

The development in v. 8 proceeds from the less important (bodily training) to the more important (godliness).

Titus 1:16a θεὸν ὁμολογοῦσιν εἰδέναι
          God   confessing   to-know
         'They profess to know God,'

16b τοῖς   **δὲ**   ἔργοις ἀρνοῦνται.
    by-the **δέ** works they-deny
    'but they deny him by their deeds;'

In Titus 1:16 the contrast marked by δέ is between τοῖς... ἔργοις ἀρνοῦνται 'by their works they deny (him)' and θεὸν ὁμολογοῦσιν εἰδέναι 'they confess to know God'. Knight (1992:303) considers the δέ in this text to be contrastive, and so does Banker (1987:62).

The argument for development here is similar to that of the previous example. The sinful nature of the Cretans was the topic of vv. 13-15. With a new point of departure in 16a Paul brings out an apparently positive foil, namely θεὸν ὁμολογοῦσιν εἰδέναι 'They confess to know God'. In 16b is another point of departure, this time τοῖς ἔργοις 'with their works', linked with δέ. Thus 16b builds on 16a and moves on to describe another sinful characteristic of the Cretans, contributing to the argument begun in vv. 13-15.

2 Tim. 2:22a τὰς δὲ   νεωτερικὰς ἐπιθυμίας φεῦγε,
           the but youthful   desires   flee
          'So shun youthful passions'

22b δίωκε **δὲ** δικαιοσύνην, πίστιν, ἀγάπην, εἰρήνην μετὰ
    pursue **δέ** righteousness faith love   peace with

τῶν ἐπικαλουμένων τὸν κύριον ἐκ καθαρᾶς καρδίας
the calling-upon   the Lord from pure   heart

'and aim at righteousness, faith, love, and peace, along with those who call upon the Lord from a pure heart.'

In 2 Tim. 2:22 is a double contrast between νεωτερικὰς ἐπιθυμίας φεῦγε 'flee youthful desires' and δίωκε δικαιοσύνην 'pursue righteousness'.

My reasoning for seeing δέ in 22b as developmental is as follows: The words in 21d, εἰς πᾶν ἔργον ἀγαθὸν ἡτοιμασμένον 'ready for every good work', have to do with righteousness as a gift, making Timothy ready for every good work. Then in 22a is a command, ἐπιθυμίας φεῦγε 'flee desires', a negative way of putting the readiness for every good work into practice. In 22b is another command, δίωκε... δικαιοσύνην 'pursue righteousness', a positive way of putting the readiness for every good work into practice (see Knight 1992:420). Righteousness as a gift (21d) is put into practice by pursuing it (22b). The foil is in 22a, on which 22b builds and from which it develops as it relates back to 21d.

2 Tim. 1:9a τοῦ σώσαντος ἡμᾶς καὶ καλέσαντος κλησει ἁγίᾳ,
the having-saved us and called with-calling holy

9b οὐ κατὰ τὰ ἔργα ἡμῶν ἀλλὰ κατὰ ἰδίαν
not according-to the work of-us but according-to personal

'who saved us and called us with a holy calling, not in virtue of our works but in virtue of his own'

πρόθεσιν καὶ χάριν, τὴν δοθεῖσαν ἡμῖν ἐν Χριστῷ
plan and grace the given to-us in Christ

Ἰησοῦ πρὸ χρόνων αἰωνίων,
Jesus before time eternal

'purpose and the grace which he gave us in Christ Jesus ages ago,'

10a φανερωθεῖσαν **δὲ** νῦν διὰ τῆς ἐπιφανείας
revealed **δέ** now through the appearance

τοῦ σωτῆρος ἡμῶν Χριστοῦ Ἰησοῦ
of-the Savior of-us Christ Jesus

'and now has manifested through the appearing of our Savior Christ Jesus'

In 2 Tim. 1:9-10a there is a double contrast: between δοθεῖσαν 'given' and φανερωθεῖσαν 'revealed', and between πρὸ χρόνων αἰωνίων 'before eternal ages' and νῦν 'now'. Knight (1992:375) describes this as a "shift" from "the grace resident in Christ to the manifestation of that grace in the appearing of Christ as the Savior...."

Along with this contrast there is also development. First, in 8-9a, Paul requests Timothy to suffer with him for the gospel, by which he has become one of God's own. Then in 9b Paul speaks of the grace given in Christ before time eternal, when it was not known to people. In 10a he indicates that this grace is revealed now in Jesus Christ as announced in the gospel (i.e., people have experienced it in their lives). Thus 10a builds on 9b, which in turn builds on 9a, relative to the topic of God's grace.

In all of the examples of this section I have demonstrated that δέ is a marker of development when it introduces a proposition. The proposition introduced by δέ always builds on a previous one and makes a significant contribution to the argument. This is true when δέ is used as a copulative (sec. 4.4.1), and it is equally true when it introduces a contrast to the preceding proposition.

4.4.3 The use of δέ in parenthetical constructions

In some texts the proposition introduced by δέ is parenthetical. In this use, δέ, although it does indicate change (so discourse linguists suggest), may, perhaps, not be developmental. Levinsohn (1992:31) himself suggests that δέ with parentheses should be considered "antidevelopmental." But in my view δέ with parentheses can well be considered developmental, though perhaps not to the same degree as elsewhere.

There is one text in the pastoral epistles that can be used to test this claim, 1 Tim. 3:4-6, which is generally considered to be a parenthesis (Knight 1992:162; Nestle, Aland, et al. 1979:553; Graham 1976:138-39). The question then is whether in this text δέ functions as a developmental marker or not. Is it true that "the information it introduces builds on what has gone before and makes a distinct contribution to the argument" (Levinsohn 1992:64)?

1 Tim. 3:4a [δεῖ ...] τοῦ ἰδίου οἴκου καλῶς προϊστάμενον
it-is-necessary the own house well overseeing
'He must manage his own household well,'

4b τέκνα ἔχοντα ἐν ὑποταγῇ, μετὰ πάσης σεμνότητος
children having in submission with all reverence
'keeping his children submissive and respectful in every way;'

5 (εἰ **δέ** τις τοῦς ἰδίου οἴκου προστῆναι οὐκ οἶδεν,
if **δέ** someone the own household to-oversee not know

πῶς ἐκκλεσίας θεοῦ ἐπιμελήσεται·)
how church of-God will-care-for
'for if a man does not know how to manage his own household, how can he care for God's church?'

6 μὴ νεόφυτον, ἵνα μὴ τυφωθεὶς
not newly-converted so-that not having-become-conceited

εἰς κρίμα ἐμπέσῃ τοῦ διαβόλου
into judgment he-fall-into of-the devil
'He must not be a recent convert, or he may be puffed up with conceit and fall into the condemnation of the devil;'

Of the commentators cited by Graham (1976:138-39), the majority consider δέ in 1 Tim. 3:5 to be contrastive. One of them, Winer (1877:566-67), understands it as causal, but notes that δέ never means 'for'.

As I look at this text with Levinsohn's definition in mind, I conclude that there is development. The proposition introduced by δέ builds on what went before, beginning with τοῦ ἰδίου οἴκου καλῶς προϊστάμενον '(it is necessary that) he oversee his own house well' in v. 4. It also adds something distinctive to the argument by restating 4a in the form of a conditional clause and ending with πῶς ἐκκλεσίας θεοῦ ἐπιμελήσεται 'how will he care for the church of God?' The only thing that is not present is the further development of the argument, since v. 6 does not build on v. 5, but returns to v. 4. It appears that the nature of a parenthesis is that development does not go beyond its border. I argue that development is present also here but only within the parenthesis.

Thus, in all of the examples of this section, δέ is a marker of development. It is developmental when used as a copula and when introducing a contrast in which case the clause it introduces functions as a foil to heighten the development marked by δέ. When δέ introduces a parenthesis, this then too is developmental.

4.5 Special uses of δέ

In this section it will be demonstrated that δέ has a developmental function in certain constructions and collocations.

4.5.1 In set constructions

In the pastoral epistles δέ is twice collocated with οὐ μόνον ... ἀλλὰ καί (1 Tim. 5:13 and 2 Tim. 4:8) and three times with μέν (2 Tim. 1:10; 2:20; 4:4).

The first of these set constructions, οὐ μόνον ... ἀλλὰ καί, eliminates the assumption characterized by μόνον 'only' while the second conjunct, introduced by ἀλλά, adds information which is not part of the previous proposition (Blass 1993:20). Blass calls this a "construction of correction" (p. 9). The question now is whether δέ functions any differently in this context than in the ones we have looked at so far. The examples that follow show that δέ does indeed maintain its basic developmental function in this context.

2 Tim. 4:7 τὸν καλὸν ἀγῶνα ἠγώνισμαι,   τὸν δρόμον τετέλεκα,
the good struggle I-have-struggled   the race I-have-run

τὴν πίστιν τετήρηκα
the faith I-have-kept

'I have fought the good fight, I have finished the race, I have kept the faith.'

8a λοιπὸν ἀπόκειταί μοι ὁ τῆς δικαιοσύνης στέφανος,
finally laid-up to-me the of-the righteousness crown

ὃν ἀποδώσει μοι ὁ κύριος ἐν ἐκείνῃ τῇ ἡμέρᾳ,
which will-give to-me the Lord in that the day

ὁ δίκαιος κριτής,
the righteous judge

'Henceforth there is laid up for me the crown of righteousness, which the Lord, the righteous judge, will award to me on that Day,'

8b **οὐ μόνον δὲ ἐμοὶ**
οὐ μόνον δέ to-me

ἀλλὰ καὶ πᾶσι τοῖς ἠγαπηκόσι τὴν ἐπιφάνειαν αὐτοῦ.
ἀλλὰ καί to-all the love the appearance of-him

'and not to me only but also to all who have loved his appearing.'

The phrase οὐ μόνον... ἀλλὰ καί in 8b eliminates the assumption that Paul alone is to receive the crown of life, while ἀλλὰ καί expands the boundary of the previous proposition by indicating that all believers will have that experience. Note that it is δέ that introduces the proposition with the set construction.

I consider δέ a developmental marker in this passage for two reasons: it introduces a construction that (1) builds on what has gone before, (in 8a) and (2) it makes a distinct contribution to the argument by enlarging the boundary (not only Paul but all God's people will receive the crown of life). (The second example of this type of construction, 1 Tim. 5:13, functions in a similar way.)

In the second set construction introduced by δέ, δέ is collocated with μέν. But μέν... δέ is rare in the New Testament.[8] In the pastoral epistles it is recorded only in 2 Timothy (BDR 1976:377). The combination can signal either a comparison or a contrast. BAGD (1979:502) indicate that at times μέν is concessive while δέ is adversative (Rom. 6:11). At other times μέν is not concessive, while δέ remains adversative (1 Cor. 1:12). Sometimes the combination of μέν... δέ simply separates one thought from another in a series without any emphasis on contrast (Rom. 14:5).[9] According to traditional scholars, δέ in this set construction can have an adversative and a copulative function. The examples of this construction in the pastoral epistles show that it is also developmental. One such example is 2 Tim. 1:10:

2 Tim. 1:10a φανερωθεῖσαν δὲ νῦν διὰ τῆς ἐπιφανείας
revealed but now through the appearance

τοῦ σωτῆρος ἡμῶν Χριστοῦ Ἰησοῦ,
of-the Savior of-us Christ Jesus

'and now has manifested through the appearing of our Savior Christ Jesus,'

10b καταργήσαντος **μὲν** τὸν θάνατον
having-destroyed μέν the death

'who abolished death'

10c φωτίσαντος **δὲ** ζωὴν καὶ ἀφθαρσίαν
having-brought-to-light δέ life and immortality

---

[8] The μέν... δέ correlation appears primarily in Acts, Paul's epistles, and Hebrews. Matthew uses it 20 times out of 491 uses of δέ, Mark three times of out 150 uses of δέ, Luke, seven times; often he uses asyndeton instead (see Luke 7:22) (Moulton and Turner 1963:331-332). Μέν is not used at all in 2 Thessalonians, 1 Timothy, Titus, 2 Peter, 1, 2, and 3 John, and Revelation (BDR 1976:377).

[9] The combination μέν οὖν... δέ does not appear in the pastoral epistles and only four times in the New Testament (Acts 12:5; 25:4, 11; 1 Cor. 9:25) (acCordance 1994). The collocation μέν οὖν denotes continuation, 'so, then' (BAGD 1979:503), while δέ introduces a developmental proposition which may be contrastive (1 Cor. 9:25) or not (Acts 25:4).

διὰ τοῦ εὐαγγελίου.
through the gospel

'and brought life and immortality to light through the gospel.'

In 2 Tim. 1:10, there is a double contrast between καταργήσαντος . . . τὸν θάνατον 'having destroyed death', on the one hand, and φωτίσαντος δὲ ζωὴν καὶ ἀφθαρσίαν 'having brought to light life and immortality', on the other. Knight (1992:376) describes this μέν . . . δέ construction as "connection and contrast."

The reasons for considering δέ as development in 2 Tim. 1:10 are as follows: While 10a speaks of the manifestation of the grace of God through the appearance (resurrection) of Jesus Christ, 10b takes the reader back to Christ's suffering and death on the cross, and then 10c returns the reader again to the risen Christ. The death of Christ (10b) is the dark background (contrast) for the risen Christ present among God's people through the gospel (10a, 10c). Thus 10c builds on 10b which intimates the death of Christ and makes a distinct contribution with the statement that he 'brought life and immortality to light through the gospel'.

Another example of the μέν . . . δέ construction is in 2 Tim. 2:20:

2 Tim. 2:19c ἀποστήτω ἀπὸ ἀδικίας
let-abstain from evil

πᾶς ὁ ὀνομάζων τὸ ὄνομα κυρίου.
everyone the naming the name of-Lord

'"Let every one who names the name of the Lord abstain from iniquity."'

20a Ἐν μεγάλῃ δὲ οἰκίᾳ οὐκ ἔστιν μόνον σκεύη
in great now house not is only vessels

χρυσᾶ καὶ ἀργυρᾶ ἀλλὰ καὶ ξύλινα καὶ ὀστράκινα,
golden and silver but also wood and clay

'In a great house there are not only vessels of gold and silver but also of wood and earthenware,'

20b καὶ ἃ **μὲν** εἰς τιμὴν
and what **μέν** into honor

'and some for noble use.'

20c ἃ **δὲ** εἰς ἀτιμίαν
what **δέ** into dishonor

'and some for ignoble.'

21 ἐὰν οὖν τις ἐκκαθάρῃ ἑαυτὸν ἀπὸ τούτων,
if then someone cleanses himself from these

ἔσται   σκεῦος εἰς τιμήν, ἡγιασμένον, εὔχρηστον
he-will-be vessel for honor sanctified   useful

τῷ   δεσπότῃ, εἰς πᾶν ἔργον ἀγαθὸν ἡτοιμασμένον.
for-the master   for every work   good   ready

'If any one purifies himself from what is ignoble, then he will be a vessel for noble use, consecrated and useful to the master of the house, ready for any good work.'

The function of δέ in 2 Tim. 2:20c is clearly developmental. Note that the Old Testament passage quoted in 19c urges God's people to abstain from wickedness. Then the implications of 20a are introduced by καί in 20b. The phrase 'some for honor' in 20b, marked as anticipatory and relatively unimportant by μέν (see Levinsohn 1992:167), refers to 'honorable vessels', the reverse of 'wickedness'. But the phrase 'some for dishonor' (in 20c), which is introduced by δέ refers back to 'wickedness' and leads right to the need for a person to cleanse himself from things that dishonor in order to become a 'vessel of honor' useful to the master (v. 21). Thus 20c, introduced by δέ, develops the point of the Old Testament quotation in 19c.

4.5.2 Collocated with other particles

The conjunction δέ sometimes occurs with καί or ἔτι:[10] δὲ καί meaning 'but also' or 'but even' (e.g., 1 Cor. 15:15); καὶ δέ meaning 'and also' or 'but also' (e.g., Acts 22:28) (BAGD 1979:171). In such combinations δέ is developmental, as the following pastoral epistles passages show:

1 Tim. 1:8 οἴδαμεν δὲ ὅτι καλὸς ὁ   νόμος
            we-know but that good the law

            ἐάν τις   αὐτῷ νομίμως χρῆται
            if someone   it   properly uses

'Now we know that the law is good, if anyone uses it lawfully,'

9a εἰδὼς   τοῦτο, ὅτι δικαίῳ   νόμος οὐ κεῖται,
    knowing this   that to-righteous law   not opposes

'understanding this, that the law is not laid down for the just'

9b ἀνόμοις   **δὲ καὶ** ἀνυποτάκτοις,
    to-lawless   <u>δὲ καὶ</u> disobedient

    ἀσεβέσι καὶ ἁμαρτωλοῖς, ἀνοσίοις καὶ βεβήλοις,
    godless and sinners   unholy   and common

    πατρολῴαις καὶ μητρολῴαις, ἀνδροφόνοις
    father-slayers and mother-slayers homocides

---

[10] According to BAGD (1979:171), ἔτι δὲ καί in the New Testament is to be translated 'and (even)' as in Acts 2:26. No denotes the addition of the content of a subordinate clause ... to that of a main clause: or vice versa' te that ἔτι does not appear in the pastoral epistles at all.

'but for the lawless and the disobedient, for the ungodly and sinners, for the unholy and profane, for murderers of fathers and murderers of mothers, for manslayers,'

In 1 Tim. 1:9 δέ introduces a single contrast, between δικαίῳ 'to righteous' and ἀνόμοις 'to lawless'. The conjunctive καί joins together ἀνόμοις and ἀνυποτάκτοις 'lawless' and 'disobedient'. The function of δέ here is clearly developmental. My reasoning is as follows: Verse 8 talks about the proper use of the law; 9a presents the foil, the improper use of the law, and then 9b introduced by δέ continues the presentation of the proper use of the law, building on and making a distinct contribution to v. 8.

1 Tim. 3:7 δεῖ   δὲ καὶ μαρτυρίαν καλὴν ἔχειν ἀπὸ τῶν ἔξωθεν,
           it-behooves δέ καί witness   good   to-have from the outside

ἵνα μὴ εἰς ὀνειδισμὸν ἐμπέσῃ καὶ παγίδα τοῦ διαβόλου.
so-that not into reproof he-fall and traps of-the devil

'moreover he must be well thought of by outsiders, or he may fall into reproach and the snare of the devil.'

In 1 Tim. 3:7 δέ is copulative. Knight (1992:164) writes that δὲ καί "together indicate that this characteristic is equally important." It adds another requirement to the list of prerequisites for an overseer. The adverbial καί here marks μαρτυρίαν καλὴν ἀπὸ τῶν ἔξωθεν 'a good testimony from the outside' for parallel processing with the other qualifications in vv. 2–6, such as μιᾶς γυναικὸς ἄνδρα 'husband of one wife'.

But the function of δέ is not only copulative, it is also developmental. My reasoning is as follows: In vv. 1–6 Paul presents requirements which are internal to the church. In v. 7 he proposes a requirement which is external to the church. The second proposition (v. 7) builds on the first (vv. 1–6) and adds distinctive contributions to it.

1 Tim. 5:24a Τινῶν   ἀνθρώπων αἱ ἁμαρτίαι πρόδηλοί εἰσιν,
            of-some people   the sins   evident   are

προάγουσαι εἰς κρίσιν,
going-before into judgment

'The sins of some men are conspicuous, pointing to judgment,'

24b τισὶν   **δὲ καὶ** ἐπακολουθοῦσιν·
    to-others δέ καί   they-follow

'but the sins of others appear later.'

There are two points of contrast between the two parts of 1 Tim. 5:24, but even so the presence of adverbial καί constrains them to parallel processing (see sec. 5.4). Though δέ in 24b appears in a context of contrast, it still functions in a developmental fashion because the previous proposition, 24a has to do with people whose sins precede them to judgment, while 24b, introduced by δέ, refers to people whose sins follow them. Thus 24b, building on 24a, makes a distinctive contribution to the argument.

The adverbial καί (BDR 1976:376) collocated with δέ is also seen in 2 Tim. 3:12:

2 Tim. 3:11b οὕς διωγμούς ὑπήνεγκα
which persecutions I-endured

καὶ ἐκ πάντων με ἐρρύσατο ὁ κύριος
and from all me rescued the Lord

'what persecutions I endured; yet from them all the Lord rescued me.'

12 **καὶ** πάντες **δὲ** οἱ θέλοντες εὐσεβῶς ζῆν
καί all **δέ** the wishing godly to-live

ἐν Χριστῷ Ἰησοῦ διωχθήσονται
in Christ Jesus will-be-persecuted

'Indeed all who desire to live a godly life in Christ Jesus will be persecuted,'

The καί in this context adds all Christians to Paul (vv. 11–12). The δέ is copulative; it leads from Paul's suffering to that of all Christians. It is also developmental; in vv. 10–11 Paul speaks of his suffering for the sake of Christ, and in v. 12 he indicates that all Christians face the same experience. Thus v. 12 builds on 11b, Paul's suffering, and makes a distinctive contribution to the argument: other Christians will suffer like Paul.

We can conclude, then, from all these examples that when δέ is collocated with καί, whether the latter precedes or follows, δέ is developmental, building on what precedes and making a distinctive contribution to the argument.

4.5.3 The difference between δέ and ἀλλά

Linguists who have described the function of δέ in terms of contrast instead of development, have had to appeal to other factors to explain how δέ differs from ἀλλά. Moulton and Turner (1963:329, 331) claim that ἀλλά is more strongly adversative than δέ. Poythress (1984:321) has a similar view. Blass (1993:18) states that ἀλλά "gives rise to a suggestion of correction or rectification," while δέ simply contrasts two conjuncts.

Once δέ is recognized as a developmental conjunction, however, the way it is different from ἀλλά is readily apparent, as Titus 1:14–15 shows:

Titus 1:14 μὴ προσέχοντες Ἰουδαϊκοῖς μύθοις καὶ
not following Jewish myths and

ἐντολαῖς ἀνθρώπων ἀποστρεφομένων τὴν ἀλήθειαν.
commands of-people perverting the truth

'instead of giving heed to Jewish myths or to commands of men who reject the truth.'

15a πάντα καθαρὰ τοῖς καθαροῖς·
    all   clean to-the clean
'To the pure all things are pure,'

15b τοῖς δὲ μεμιαμμένοις καὶ ἀπίστοις οὐδὲν καθαρόν,
    to-the <u>δέ</u> defiled   and unbelieving nothing clean

ἀλλὰ μεμίανται αὐτῶν καὶ ὁ νοῦς καὶ ἡ συνείδησις.
<u>ἀλλά</u> is-defiled of-them and the mind and the conscience
'but to the corrupt and unbelieving nothing is pure; their very minds and consciences are corrupted.'

I see δέ as developmental in Titus 1:15b for the following reasons: v. 14 provides a negative witness about the Cretan life and behavior; 15a with its fronted πάντα καθαρά 'all things are clean' provides a foil for what follows in that it records a positive statement; and 15b, introduced by δέ, builds on 15a as it returns to the negative characteristics of 14, expanding on them until v. 16.

But with what does ἀλλά in 15b contrast? It appears right after οὐδὲν καθαρόν 'nothing is clean' in that it follows the general pattern described in chapter 2. That is, the first assumption is denied and a second one is put in its place (Blass 1993:18). In this context ἀλλά introduces intensification, not contrast: not only is nothing clean but their mind and conscience are defiled. While there is a contrast, the context requires that ἀλλά be translated 'in fact'. Knight (1992:303) states that "ἀλλά is a further enlargement of the contrast already begun with δέ, as the repetition of the main verb μιαίνω bears out."

4.6 Conclusion

Though traditional scholars maintain that δέ has two basic functions, contrastive and copulative, they themselves intimate that the contrastive function may be basic and that the copulative function comes into play only when no difference exists between the two clauses which δέ conjoins. In this way they anticipated modern linguistic research.

In line with the intimation of the former and the conclusion of the latter, I have in this chapter demonstrated that δέ has a single function, neither contrastive nor copulative, nor, for that matter, introducing only change, but marking development. If δέ functions as a copula, it marks a proposition as a development of a previous one. If it introduces a contrast, the proposition introduced by δέ builds on the preceding conjunct as a foil, as it makes its distinctive contribution to the proposition prior to the foil. Even when δέ occurs in some set construction, it does not lose its basic developmental function.

While Levinsohn is reluctant to claim that parenthetical δέ is also developmental, I have demonstrated that it displays developmental features with one exception, viz. that development ends at the border of the parenthesis. Thus δέ is developmental in all the texts that I surveyed. I therefore conclude that, in some sense, δέ is always developmental.

5 Adverbial Καί As a Marker of Addition

The particle καί has two different though related functions. One of them, to be covered in chapter 6, is its function as a conjunction, uniting two propositions usually of the same level or span. Its other function Blass describes as "constraint on relevance." Titrud calls it "the adverbial καί." This function, which appears to have been its original use, is the one which I address in this chapter.

Since the same morpheme had two different functions, native speakers needed to have a way to distinguish between them. As a conjunction, καί almost invariably links contiguous constituents. If it occurs at the beginning of a clause, it is normally conjoining contiguous clauses. Adverbial καί, in contrast, links noncontiguous constituents across clause or sentence boundaries. It frequently is found clause-internal since it immediately precedes the constituent which it is adding to an earlier one. If it stands at the beginning of a clause, it is still easily recognizable, since it usually precedes a postpositional conjunction such as γάρ or δέ.[1]

As will be shown, adverbial καί is additive just like conjunctive καί, but joins clause constituents across clause boundaries rather than within a clause. Its major function is to create a parallel-processing constraint on words, phrases, and clauses marked by it (Blass 1993:13). In sections 5.1–5.3, I survey the views of traditional and discourse linguists to uncover a possible common thread in their understanding of adverbial καί that might point to its having a single function. Then in section 5.4 evidence is presented that the pastoral epistles literature does in fact support a single function.

5.1 How traditional scholars of Classical Greek view the adverbial καί

In their view of the adverbial καί, Liddell and Scott identify three distinct functions. Denniston, at the other end, recognizes a single basic function from which a second is derived. Smyth and KG are somewhere between.

According to Liddell and Scott (1940:857–58), adverbial καί has an ascensive function translated 'even' (in Homer's *Iliad* 11.654), an additive function translated 'also' (in Xenophon's *Anabasis* 2.6.30), and a limiting function translated 'just' (in Sophocles's *Ajax* 1290). It influences whole clauses or single words. It appears frequently in main clauses after temporal conjunctions

---

[1] Denniston (1954:325) points out that in the collocation δὲ καί, the adverbial καί usually comes after the first word in the clause and before the emphatic word, except when this word is preceded by an article or a preposition.

(in Homer's *Iliad* 1.494).² A condition represented as an extreme case is introduced by καί εἰ translated 'even if' (in Homer's *Iliad* 4.37). In the reverse order, εἰ καί, the meaning is 'although, notwithstanding that'. In both of these, καί affects the whole clause, not just one word. It can also appear before a participle which represents εἰ καί or καί εἰ (in Homer's *Iliad* 9.655). It is used with adverbs to give emphasis (in Herodotus 6.125) and with words expressing a minimum (in Homer's *Odyssey* 1.58). (Denniston has a clarifying note regarding the last two uses: "'Even' then passes into 'actually', and καί is little more than a particle of emphasis, like δή [certainly, indeed]." In sum, then, Liddell and Scott claim that adverbial καί has an ascensive function, an additive function, and a limiting function, and it affects whole clauses or single words.

Smyth (1956:652) sees the number of functions which adverbial καί performs as two: additive 'also' and ascensive 'even'. He notes that adverbial καί "stresses an important idea," usually presented by the word which follows but sometimes by the one which precedes when it stands as the first word in the clause.

While KG (1955, Vol. 1, pp. 253–54) agree with Smyth about the number of functions, they point out that the additive function is basic. According to them, the primary meaning of the adverbial καί is 'also', adding a new constituent or thought to a preceding one: Socrates was wise, καί Plato was wise. The ascensive meaning 'even' was separate from the additive meaning and came later, often characterized by the presence of οὐ μόνον, ὥσπερ καί, or εἴπερ καί.

Denniston (1954) agrees with KG and Smyth, adding that the two uses which they present were common in all periods and styles of Greek literature. While he appears to contradict KG's claim that additive was first, he suggests that climax derived from addition: "when the addition is surprising, or difficult of acceptance, and when a sense of climax is present, 'also' becomes 'even'" (p. 293). He says, helpfully, "καί everywhere denotes the connexion between two ideas, either expressed or fairly clearly implied" (p. 316).

The general consensus, then, is that adverbial καί has two functions, additive 'also' and ascensive 'even' (KG, Denniston, Smyth), but with the ascensive use in some way derived from the additive one. A third function, limiting, translated as 'just', is advanced only by Liddell and Scott and appears to be incorrect. KG's position that of the two functions the additive was original is in harmony with Denniston's suggestion that climax is derived from addition. Thus KG and Denniston clearly lean towards seeing one basic function: addition.

5.2 How traditional scholars of New Testament Greek view the adverbial καί

Since the Greek of the New Testament has its roots in Classical Greek, the conclusions of KG and Denniston, which tend towards one basic function of

---

² "... it denotes the addition of the content of a subordinate clause ... to that of a main clause: or vice versa" (Denniston 1954:294).

adverbial καί, have great significance for the New Testament literature as well: the examples in the pastoral epistles support this view.

However, the traditional scholars of New Testament Greek do not offer this understanding of adverbial καί. BAGD, for example, cite multiple functions: additive, ascensive, and "pleonastic." According to BAGD (1979), adverbial καί sometimes functions as an adverb with the meaning of 'also, likewise' (Luke 21:31). When it appears between alternate names (Saul καί Paul), it may be translated 'who is also called' (Acts 13:9). When it is used with a relative pronoun, it often gives greater independence to the following relative clause (Gal. 2:10). In certain contexts it is used with ascensive force and can be translated 'even' (Eph. 5:12). After an interrogative it can be translated 'at all, still'[3] (1 Cor. 15:29). In sentences that indicate comparison, it appears variously, sometimes in both members of the comparison, "often, pleonastically, to our way of thinking" (Rom. 5:19). It also introduces expressions of cause or result, 'for this reason (also)', which is "pleonastic to a considerable degree" (2 Cor. 2:9). It can be used pleonastically with prepositions as well (Phil. 4:3) (p. 393).

BAGD's view of καί, then, while similar to that of KG, Smyth, and Denniston who see its function as additive ('also'), and ascensive ('even'), does not tend towards a single basic function. And though BAGD do not mention Liddell and Scott's limiting function, 'just', they do refer to a "pleonastic" function, making three functions.

5.3 How discourse linguists view the adverbial καί in the New Testament

Now we turn to the views of two discourse linguists. Blass (1993) proposes a dual function for καί, viz. parallel processing and confirmation. Titrud (1991) subscribes to a unitary function, viz. prominence. (In describing the function of καί in this section I use the term *adverbial* καί, following Titrud.)

Blass (1993) sees the adverbial καί as a use that is a constraint on relevance, and she says it "can be divided into two 'the parallel' and 'the confirmatory use'" (p. 13). She says that in the parallel use καί usually follows the item it relates to and precedes the item it constrains to parallel processing. She points to Rom. 16:1-2, an introduction of Phoebe as sister and deaconess to the Roman Christians, as an example where the preceding parallel is either stated (see v. 1) or merely implied (see v. 2):

> (v. 1) Now I present to you Phoebe, our sister, being [καί] a deaconess of the church of Cenchrea,
> (v. 2) so that you might receive her in the Lord worthy of saints and provide her with whatever she needs from you, καί for she herself [αὐτή] was a helper of many and of me myself.

---

[3] Denniston (1954:313) considers such a construction a "descending climax" with the translation *at all, to start with*.

According to Blass (pp. 8-9) the adverbial καί preceding the term διάκονος[4] indicates that this designation of Phoebe is to be processed with an earlier designation of her, namely ἀδελφή 'sister', meaning a fellow Christian. Both propositions provide reasons for Paul's directive about her to the church in Rome. The second καί constrains αὐτή to indicate that Phoebe among others provided support for many people including Paul. These "others" are not mentioned but implied.

Blass supports her "confirmatory use" (p. 10) with a reference to 2 Cor. 5:2-4 (v. 1 is cited here to provide the context):

(v. 1) γάρ we know that if the earthly tent we live in is destroyed, we have a building from God, a house not made with hands, eternal in the heavens.
(v. 2) καὶ γάρ here we groan, and long to put on our heavenly dwelling,
(v. 3) so that καί by putting it on, we may not be found naked.
(v. 4) καὶ γάρ while we are still in this tent we sigh with anxiety . . .

Blass insists, "It is quite impossible to translate καί any other way in these contexts than as a confirmatory particle, since there is no parallel to be found" (p. 11). But this is not the case. According to Hodge (1859), "the words καὶ γάρ may mean . . . 'for also' . . ." Since v. 2 is coordinate with v. 1, it provides an additional reason why the apostle looked at the things unseen and eternal. Bernard ([1906] 1967) considers that "vv. 2, 3 and vs. 4 form two parallel sentences." Thus in both v. 2 and v. 4, καί provides a parallel processing constraint on the word or phrase after γάρ.

Blass notes further that the constraint function of καί can at times be translated as 'even'. She considers that this meaning arises out of the context of "lowness of likelihood" and is not part of the meaning of adverbial καί (p. 12). (Compare this view to Denniston's derivation of climax from addition, discussed near the end of sec. 5.1.). Blass claims that in such a context καί is employed both in a parallel way (Rom. 5:7, for on behalf of a good person perhaps someone καί dares to die) and in a confirmatory way (2 Cor. 4:3, if [εἰ] δὲ καί[5] our gospel is covered, it is covered among those who are perishing). However, in 2 Cor. 4:3, the presence of δέ constrains v. 3 to be interpreted as a new development in the argument, not as confirmation of an earlier point of the argument. In turn, καί may be interpreted as constraining 'if our gospel is covered' to be processed in parallel with the earlier statement that the truth of the gospel was being proclaimed openly (v. 2).

Blass (1993:12) supports a third use for καί, namely an additive one. (This use is different from what Denniston calls additive, which is simply 'also'.) Blass translates an "additive" καί as 'still, in addition to' as in Rom 8:24 (But

---

[4] Though there are a number of manuscripts that omit the adverbial καί, its presence is supported by p[46] and B, whose importance far outweighs the omission by the other manuscripts. Further, some of the important manuscripts in favor of omission were corrected or are corrections.

[5] BAGD consider εἰ καί to be a special construction, meaning 'even if, even though, although' (1979:220; cf. BDR 1976:305).

hope seen is not hope, for who [καί] hopes for what he sees).[6] At the close of her treatment of the additive καί Blass notes, "In Greek . . . 'in addition to' is due to the context, just as it is with 'even' and it is not due to the meaning of the particle." In other words, the function of καί (assuming that it is accepted as part of the Rom. 8:24 text) is still to constrain parallel processing.

In my view, only one of the functions that Blass proposes is tenable: the parallel use. The confirmatory use of καί she derived from the presence of γάρ or its synonym διό 'wherefore', both of which are confirmatory. To see the function of adverbial καί as parallel and only parallel agrees with what Denniston says: ". . . καί everywhere denotes the connexion between two ideas, either expressed or fairly clearly implied" (p. 316).

Titrud (1991) describes the function of adverbial καί primarily in terms of prominence. He says that adverbial καί calls special attention to what follows and marks it with prominence (Mark 4:41, *even* the wind and the waves . . .). It can express bewilderment (John 7:47, did he deceive you *too*?), extremity (Matt. 10:30, *even* the hairs of your head; Gal. 5:12, *even* castrate themselves), and make a strong assertion (2 Pet. 1:5, for this *very* reason). He states that it "appears that the primary function of the adverbial καί is to indicate that the following component(s) should be intensified or emphasized just as a spotlight focuses our attention on something" (p. 4). When one element is intensified, he claims (p. 6), καί is often rendered 'also, even' to indicate that another element present is not singled out. The adverbial καί in 1 Pet. 3:19, for example, should be translated, 'He went *even* to the spirits in prison who formerly disobeyed' (p. 7).

Titrud maintains (p. 5) that the particle carries emotive overtones as well. The precise nature of the overtone depends on the context. In Luke 13:7, for instance, it should be translated 'Why should it use up *valuable* ground?' Here καί intensifies 'ground' and marks it as important, he says, but without evidence in support of it, other than citing the Phillips translation of Luke 13:7.

Titrud does not describe adverbial καί in terms of "addition to the context of the preceding" (Denniston 1954:293; cf. KG 1955, Vol. 2, p. 253), but only in terms of the constituent that immediately follows καί, whether this is a word, a phrase, or a clause. Thus concerning 1 Pet. 2:21 he writes, "The focus is on the fact that *even Christ Himself suffered,* so that they also should endure suffering" (p. 6).

Even in occurrences of the correlative καί . . . καί, Titrud (1992:244–45) considers the first καί to be an intensifier (the second being the conjunction), as in Matt. 10:28: καὶ ψυχὴν καὶ σῶμα 'both soul and body'. Of this he says, "The

---

[6] The Nestle-Aland text does not have καί here; it is a variant reading adopted by some editions of the Greek New Testament on the basis of somewhat weak manuscript support: $\aleph^2$ A C Ψ M b sy^h sa; Cl.

When Denniston (1954:293) makes reference to an "addition to the content of the preceding," he appears to refer to the basic function of the particle and not to some "additive" use.

first καί in the construction ... is the adverb, stressing the inclusion of each of the two items specified."

Now it is true that adverbial καί does at times appear in the context of intensification (i.e., it is ascensive). Both Denniston (1954:293) and Blass (1993:12) recognize this. Many passages which Titrud cites are of this type. But in other passages it is not obvious that the author has more than addition in mind, as in 1 Tim. 5:20: Reprove, in the presence of all, the ones who are sinning, so that καί the rest may have fear. In this text the focus is not primarily on 'the rest' but on 'fear', since 'have fear' is new information and is a comment about the topic '(they plus) the rest'.

Titrud appears to bypass concern for constituent order, even though many examples of adverbial καί involve fronting—placing a constituent before the verb (Levinsohn 1992:18). Note that fronting may be used not only to emphasize or highlight a constituent, but also to provide a "point of departure" (p. 13). Levinsohn defines a point of departure as "a fronted constituent placed at the beginning of a clause or sentence both to set a 'domain' for what follows ... and to provide a primary basis for relating what follows to the context" (p. 18).

In the case of 1 Tim. 5:20, the point of departure is 'the rest', marked by adverbial καί for parallel processing with 'the ones who are sinning' as people who will have fear. The adverbial καί in this text is better understood as additive, not ascensive as Titrud seems to say: "καί... marks what is prominent" (1991:5). What is prominent is 'have fear', which is new information.

However, I agree with Titrud (loc. cit.) when he rejects pleonasm, saying, "There is a pragmatic difference between the use of καί and its nonuse, even though it may be slight." There are two reasons for this: First, the presence of καί requires more processing time and so calls attention to what it introduces. Second, since the author used a καί, though he could have used asyndeton, he must have had a purpose for it.

To sum up, then, Titrud rejects pleonasm as an explanation for adverbial καί and rightly so. But his claim that the particle marks primarily prominence appears untenable. Blass has proposed two basic functions, one she calls parallel processing use and the other confirmatory. However, as I have demonstrated, the confirmatory use is most likely a misunderstanding of the cited texts. The parallel-processing use/function has three manifestations, according to Blass: a simple processing one, 'also'; a 'lowness of likelihood' one 'even'; and an additive one, 'still, in addition to'. She indicates clearly, though, that the last two are context determined. The parallel-processing use is the only one that reflects the basic function of adverbial καί.

Blass's parallel-processing approach appears to me to be viable for the following reasons: KG and Denniston mention only two functions for adverbial καί, additive 'also' and ascensive 'even'. KG claim that the ascensive followed the additive and was dependent on it. Denniston explains how the ascensive developed from the additive and also indicates that adverbial "καί everywhere denotes the connexion between two ideas." This is precisely what Blass proposes, as I understand it; only she goes further. It is not only a matter of connection between two ideas, but a parallel relationship of one constituent with another whether stated or implied. This approach seems to me to be the most promising one for understanding adverbial καί and is the one I argue for in the next section.

5.4 The use of adverbial καί in the pastoral Epistles

Adverbial καί, which appears twenty-four times in the pastoral epistles (acCordance 1994), functions everywhere as a constraint on relevance (Blass 1993:7). Its occurrences in the pastoral epistles demonstrate that adverbial καί constrains an immediately following word, phrase, or clause to parallel processing with a preceding word, phrase, or clause, whether stated or implied. The various effects of using adverbial καί are determined by the context.[7] It is unfortunate that no examples of "ascensive" καί showing "lowness of likelihood" occur in the pastoral epistles. (For examples elsewhere in the New Testament, see sec. 5.3.)

5.4.1 Same subject, different complement

In the example that follows, the adverbial καί marks the complement for parallel processing with an earlier complement, while the subject remains the same.

1 Tim. 2:5 εἷς γὰρ θεός, εἷς **καὶ** μεσίτης
one for God one **καὶ** mediator

θεοῦ καὶ ἀνθρώπων, ἄνθρωπος Χριστὸς Ἰησοῦς
of-God and men man Christ Jesus

'For there is one God, and there is one mediator between God and men, the man Christ Jesus.'

In 1 Tim. 2:5 μεσίτης 'mediator'[8] is marked by καί for parallel processing (see Graham 1976:84–85). The statement εἷς καὶ μεσίτης θεοῦ καὶ ἀνθρώπων 'one is also the mediator between God and men' implies that someone else is εἷς 'one'. Here the other εἷς 'one' is explicit in the previous clause; it is θεός 'God'. Paul marks μεσίτης for parallel processing with θεός. As for prominence, it is the uniqueness both of the Father and of the mediator that is stressed, not the constituent 'mediator', since the subject 'one' is fronted and repeated. Knight appears to make the same point (1992:121): "Just as there is only one God, so there is only one mediator...." A little later he adds, "The one God has

---

[7] Adverbial καί in οὐ μόνον δέ ... ἀλλὰ καί is discussed in chapter 4.

[8] The Greek is ambiguous. I use the term *complement* on the basis of the normal English translation, 'There is one mediator...' If 'God' and 'mediator' are taken as subject of their respective clauses, καί would still be marking parallel processing.

provided one mediator between himself (θεός) and humans (ἀνθρώπων, plural)...."

2 Tim. 1:11 εἰς ὃ ἐτέθην ἐγὼ κῆρυξ
for which I-was-made myself herald

καὶ ἀπόστολος καὶ διδάσκαλος.
and apostle and teacher
'For this gospel I was appointed a preacher and apostle and teacher,'

12 δι' ἣν αἰτίαν **καὶ** ταῦτα πάσχω,
for which reason <u>καί</u> these I-suffer

ἀλλ' οὐκ ἐπαισχύνομαι, οἶδα γὰρ ᾧ πεπίστευκα,
but not I-am-ashamed I-know for whom I-have-believed

καὶ πέπεισμαι ὅτι δυνατός ἐστιν τὴν παραθήκην μου
and I-trust that able he-is the deposit of-me

φυλάξαι εἰς ἐκείνην τὴν ἡμέραν
to-guard for that the day

'and therefore I suffer as I do. But I am not ashamed, for I know whom I have believed, and I am sure that he is able to guard until that Day what has been entrusted to me.'

Knight (1992:378) says that the phrase "δι' ἣν αἰτίαν functions as a causal conjunction with the meaning 'for which reason, therefore'" (cf. BAGD 1979:26). It gives the ground for Paul's suffering, namely that he is a herald, an apostle, and a teacher of the gospel. He indicates what he suffers with the demonstrative ταῦτα 'these things'. What these things are, he does not mention, though he most likely refers to his imprisonment (cf. v. 8). Καί marks the complement ταῦτα for parallel processing with a corresponding construction. In addition to what Paul has suffered in the past, he also suffers 'these things' (see Minor 1992:29).

5.4.2 Same subject, different verb

In the following passage the adverbial καί is used twice to mark a verb for parallel processing with an earlier verb that is different.

2 Tim. 2:11a πιστὸς ὁ λόγος·
faithful the word
'This saying is sure:'

11b εἰ γὰρ συναπεθάνομεν,
if for we-died-with

καὶ συζήσομεν·
<u>καί</u> we-will-live-with

'If we have died with him, we shall also live with him;'

12a εἰ ὑπομένομεν,
    if we-endure-with

    καὶ συμβασιλεύσομεν·
    <u>καὶ</u> we-will-rule-with

    'if we endure, we shall also reign with him;'

Here is one of those "faithful sayings" which Paul uses frequently in the pastoral epistles. In it γάρ (11b) introduces the following propositions as an explanation of πιστὸς ὁ λόγος 'faithful the word'.

The clauses συζήσομεν 'we will live with' and συμβασιλεύσομεν 'we will rule with' are each marked by καί for parallel processing. For συζήσομεν the parallel is συναπεθάνομεν; for συμβασιλεύσομεν it is ὑπομένομεν. Since the parallel is obvious even without καί, Paul may convey something more with the use of καί. Knight (1992:404–5) suggests that this "more" is emphasis: "Adverbial καί throws emphasis on συζήσομεν" and "it lays emphasis on the future 'reigning with Christ'." Titrud's claim (1991:4) that adverbial καί here marks prominence may have validity. A second possibility is that καί here indicates that 'living' is *added* to 'dying', and 'ruling' to 'enduring', rather than being *contrasted* with them.

5.4.3 Different subject, same verb

In the following passage the adverbial καί marks a different subject for parallel processing.

1 Tim 5:20a τοὺς ἁμαρτάνοντας ἐνώπιον πάντων ἔλεγχε,
    the ones-sinning before all reprove

    'As for those who persist in sin, rebuke them in the presence of all,'

20b ἵνα   **καὶ** οἱ λοιποὶ φόβον ἔχωσιν.
    so-that <u>καὶ</u> the rest fear may-have

    'so that the rest may stand in fear.'

In 1 Tim. 5:20 Timothy is directed to reprove τοὺς ἁμαρτάνοντας 'the ones sinning' in the presence of all. The adverbial καί marks οἱ λοιποί 'the rest' for parallel processing with τοὺς ἁμαρτάνοντας (see Graham 1976:292). The τοὺς ἁμαρτάνοντας come to fear the power of sin through reproof. The οἱ λοιποί who are present for the public reproof will be affected as well. Thus καί ties together 'the rest' and 'the ones sinning', both having been rebuked and both coming to fear.

The next example is another part of the "faithful saying" referred to in section 5.4.2.

2 Tim. 2:12 εἰ ἀρνησόμεθα,
    if we-will-deny

κἀκεῖνος [καί ἐκεῖνος] ἀρνήσεται ἡμᾶς.
καί that-one will-deny us
'if we deny him, he also will deny us'

In 2 Tim. 2:12 the adverbial καί constrains the point of departure (ἐκεῖνος 'that-one') plus the verb (ἀρνήσεται 'he will deny') for parallel processing with ἀρνησόμεθα ('we will deny'). What is prominent is the predicate, since ἐκεῖνος is fronted as a point of departure. (This is how Knight [1992:406] appears to take the sentence, when he translates it "If we deny him, he also will deny us.")

2 Tim. 2:2a καὶ ἃ ἤκουσας παρ' ἐμοῦ διὰ πολλῶν μαρτύρων,
and what you-heard from me through many witnesses
'and what you heard from me before many witnesses'

2b ταῦτα παράθου πιστοῖς ἀνθρώποις,
these set-before faithful men
'entrust to faithful men'

2c οἵτινες ἱκανοὶ ἔσονται καὶ ἑτέρους διδάξαι.
who sufficient will-be καί others to-teach
'who will be able to teach others also.'

What Timothy had heard from Paul through many witnesses he was to transmit to other men. They were to be people of a special kind, such as could teach others (ἑτέρους). This is what καί as a parallel processing marker before ἑτέρους brings out. Timothy was to instruct Christian leaders; they in turn would teach others, especially future leaders (Knight 1992:392; Minor 1992:46). The parallel is between ἑτέρους 'others' and πιστοῖς ἀνθρώποις 'faithful men'. Thus the objects of the action are different. While the verbs are not identical, they are nevertheless synonymous.[9]

5.4.4 Different subject, same predicate

In the following passage the adverbial καί marks a different subject for parallel processing with the previous one. Each subject has the same predicate, 'are good', explicitly stated.

1 Tim. 5:24 Τινῶν ἀνθρώπων αἱ ἁμαρτίαι πρόδηλοί εἰσιν,
of-some people the sins evident are

προάγουσαι εἰς κρίσιν, τισὶν δὲ καὶ ἐπακολουθοῦσιν·
going-before into judgment to-some but also they-follow-after
'The sins of some men are conspicuous, pointing to judgment, but the sins of others appear later.'

---

[9] According to Denniston (1954:294), "καί emphasizes the fact that the relative clause contains an addition to the information contained in the main clause."

25 ὡσαύτως   καὶ τὰ ἔργα τὰ καλὰ πρόδηλα,
in-the-same-way καὶ the works the good evident
καὶ τὰ ἄλλως   ἔχοντα κρυβῆναι οὐ δύνανται.
and the otherwise having to-be-hid not they-are-able

'So also good deeds are conspicuous; and even when they are not, they cannot remain hidden.'

Not only are the *sins* of some people evident (πρόδηλοι) (v. 24), the τὰ ἔργα τὰ καλά 'works, the good ones' are evident as well. Hence τὰ ἔργα τὰ καλά is marked for parallel processing with αἱ ἁμαρτίαι 'the sins' (of some people). Notice that καί is contiguous to ὡσαύτως 'in the same way, similarly, likewise' (BAGD 1979:899), which marks the structural parallel between the two sentences; καί (which is not obligatory with ὡσαύτως)[10] indicates which specific word or phrase is marked for parallel processing.

5.4.5 The correlative καί . . . καί

Denniston (1954:323) writes concerning correlative καί . . . καί, "Normally the first καί is preparatory (i.e., adverbial), the second connective (i.e., conjunctive): 'both . . . and'." This means that, in a correlative construction, the adverbial καί looks forward rather than backward. Usually the adverbial καί marks the constituent it introduces for parallel processing with a corresponding constituent previously stated or implied. In correlative καί . . . καί, however, the adverbial καί marks the conjunct it introduces for parallel processing with the constituent joined by the conjunctive καί. The following is an example:

Titus 1:15 πάντα καθαρὰ τοῖς   καθαροῖς·
           all   clean   to-the clean

τοῖς   δὲ μεμιαμμένοις καὶ ἀπίστοις
to-the but defiled   and unbelieving

οὐδὲν   καθαρόν, ἀλλὰ μεμίανται
nothing clean   but   they-are-defiled

αὐτῶν **καὶ** ὁ   νοῦς **καὶ** ἡ   συνείδησις.
their   καί   the mind καί   the conscience

'To the pure all things are pure, but to the corrupt and unbelieving nothing is pure; their very minds and consciences are corrupted.'

Normally, καί before ὁ νοῦς 'the mind' would mark it for parallel processing with a previous noun phrase. The preceding αὐτῶν blocks this. Instead the

---

[10] This particle is used seventeen times in the New Testament; it calls attention to a formal parallel (cf. 1 Tim. 3:8; Titus 2:3, 6). It appears six times with καί, which indicates what specifically is parallel (Mark 14:31; Luke 20:3; Rom. 8:26; 1 Cor. 11:25; 1 Tim. 2:9; 5:25) (macBible 1988).

presence of conjunctive καί confirms that ὁ νοῦς is to undergo parallel processing with ἡ συνείδησις 'the conscience'.[11]

5.4.6 The collocation of δέ with καί

My goal in this section is to demonstrate that the adverbial καί functions as a constraint for parallel processing when it is collocated with δέ just as in the other contexts already examined. Two passages in the pastoral epistles illustrate this.

1 Tim. 5:24a Τινῶν   ἀνθρώπων   αἱ   ἁμαρτίαι   πρόδηλοί εἰσιν,
of-some   people   the   sins   evident   are

προάγουσαι εἰς κρίσιν,
preceding   into judgment

'The sins of some men are conspicuous, pointing to judgment,'

24b τισὶν **δὲ καὶ** ἐπακολουθοῦσιν.
others **δὲ καί** they-follow-after

'but the sins of other appear later.'

25 ὡσαύτως   καὶ τὰ ἔργα   τὰ καλὰ πρόδηλα,
in-the-same-way   also the works the good manifest

καὶ τὰ ἄλλως   ἔχοντα κρυβῆναι οὐ δύνανται.
and the otherwise having to-be-hid not they-are-able

'So also the good deeds are conspicuous; and even when they are not, they cannot remain hidden.'

In 1 Tim. 5:24 there is a double contrast: τινῶν ἀνθρώπων αἱ ἁμαρτίαι προάγουσαι 'the sins of some precede' is contrasted with τισὶν... ἐπακολουθοῦσιν 'others they follow'. Here δέ is a marker of development (see chap. 4). In v. 25 there is yet another contrast: the visibility of τὰ ἔργα τὰ καλά 'the good works' is contrasted with good works done in secret. This verse is marked by ὡσαύτως and by καί for parallel processing (cf. 1 Tim. 5:24–25 in sec. 5.4.4). Because v. 25 is parallel with both parts of v. 24, the second half of v. 24 is marked for parallel processing with the first half.

2 Tim. 2:4 οὐδεὶς στρατευόμενος ἐμπλέκεται
no-one being-soldier   gets-involved-in

ταῖς τους βίου πραγματείαις
the of-the life matters

ἵνα τῷ στρατολογήσαντι   ἀρέσῃ
so-that the having-become-commander he-may-please

---

[11] Knight (1992:303) notes that the καί... καί construction "closely links 'mind' and 'conscience'" in Titus 1:15.

'No soldier on service gets entangled in civilian pursuits, since his aim is to satisfy the one who enlisted him.'

5 ἐὰν **δὲ καὶ** ἀθλῇ   τις,
  if δὲ καί engage-in-contest someone

οὐ στεφανοῦται   ἐὰν μὴ νομίμως ἀθλήσῃ.
not he-will-be-crowned if not lawfully he-engages-in-contest

'An athlete is not crowned unless he competes according to the rules.'

In 2 Tim. 2:4 δέ is developmental in function. The proposition it introduces builds on what precedes, a teaching point based on the example of a soldier, and makes a distinct contribution, a different teaching point drawn from the example of an athlete (Minor 1992:49). The adverbial καί marks ἀθλῇ τις 'someone engages in a contest' for parallel processing with οὐδεὶς στρατευόμενος ἐμπλέκεται 'no one being a soldier gets involved'. It is an indication that the second teaching point is closely tied with the first (Knight 1992:394).

These two passages in the pastoral epistles show that the basic function of adverbial καί is to mark a word, phrase, or clause for parallel processing even when the developmental marker δέ is present.

5.5 Conclusion

Throughout the pastoral epistles the basic function of adverbial καί is to mark the word, phrase, or clause which immediately follows it for parallel processing. My analysis of the examples of καί in the pastoral epistles confirms Titrud's view that pleonastic is never a valid classification for καί, but not his claim that adverbial καί usually marks the constituent that follows it for prominence. My analysis confirms half of Blass's claims concerning adverbial καί and largely parallels Denniston's position, that the 'additive' function of καί is primary.

6 Conjunctive Καί As a Marker of Addition

In chapter 5 it was demonstrated that adverbial καί usually constrains parallel processing between noncontiguous constituents, whether the first constituent is stated or assumed. In this chapter it will be demonstrated that conjunctive καί is a marker of addition between contiguous constituents. It unites both formally equal and formally unequal constituents into a larger constituent.

Translators and commentators frequently do not know what to do with certain uses of καί. Often they seem unaware of the distinctive uses and consider them redundant and therefore omit καί from their translations or comments. Some traditional Greek scholars even describe some uses of καί as pleonastic (i.e., redundant). Discourse linguists, however, hold that καί was not used arbitrarily, but has a specific function in a discourse. I intend to demonstrate in this chapter that καί is meaningful wherever it is used.

Section 6.1 is a look at the view of Classical Greek scholars to determine what meaning and function they ascribe to καί. In sections 6.2 and 6.3 I consider the views of New Testament linguists. In section 6.4 I demonstrate from the pastoral epistles data that conjunctive καί functions as a marker of addition between contiguous constituents, whether formally equal or unequal,[1] constraining the processing of the following material as an addition to, and not as a development of, what precedes.

6.1 How traditional scholars of Classical Greek view καί

In Classical Greek literature the conjunctive καί is considered by scholars to function as a copulative, joining words, phrases, clauses, or sentences. Its gloss is 'and' in most cases. Its basic function is addition.

According to Liddell and Scott, the first major function of καί is conjoining. It joins a word or sentence to the one that immediately precedes it, (as in Homer's *Iliad* 1:528: καί with dark-blue eyebrows Zeus nodded). Or it can add an appositive expression limiting or defining the referent (as in *Hymn to Apollo* 17: to a great mountain, καί [namely] the Cynthian hill).

Liddell and Scott's second function is when καί occurs at the beginning of a sentence: in appeals or requests (Homer's *Iliad*: 23:75, καί give your hand to me); and in questions when it is used to introduce an objection or express surprise (Aeschylus's *Agamemnon* 280: Pray καί [and], who may accomplish the swiftness of messengers?) It sometimes appears at the beginning of a speech (Lysias's *Fragments* 36a). It can even function as an equivalent of καίτοι 'and yet' (Aristophanes's *Equites* 1245).

---

[1] For the use of καί with δέ, ἀλλά, and οὖν, see the chapters dealing with these conjunctions.

The third function of καί, according to Liddell and Scott, is when καί occurs after words implying sameness or likeness and means 'as' (Herodotus 7.50: they had the same opinion καί [as] you). When used in this way it may appear after words of comparison or opposition (Thucydides 7.28: the expenses were not καί [like] formerly). It may also be used to express simultaneity (Sophocles's *Philoctetes* 355: it was the second καί [and] I myself came to land)

Liddell and Scott's fourth function of καί is joining an affirmative clause with a following negative one (Sophocles's *Trachiniae* 160: but he crawled in order to do something καί not to die). Their fifth is to suggest a loose definition of number 'about' (Herodotus 2.60, 68: καί toward seventy-thousand). And the sixth is when καί is used with anacoluthon (Homer's *Iliad* 22:247: so saying, καί cunningly Athena led (Liddell and Scott 1940:857).

The last function of καί listed by Liddell and Scott is in the correlative καί ... καί 'not only ... but also' (Plato's *Gorgias* 523a).[2] Smyth (1956:651) notes that the καί ... καί construction "emphasizes each member separately, and forms a less close combination than τὲ ... καί."

Regarding Liddell and Scott's analysis it should be said that their second function has to do with a clause which either is joined to the preceding clause or is a response to something that was said or requested. In other words, this is a function in which conjunctive καί marks the addition of a constituent to a contiguous constituent. Alternately, the constituent so marked is added to a parallel one implied in the immediate context (i.e., καί is adverbial). Liddell and Scott's third function also has to do with conjoining or addition. Their fifth one appears to me to be more adverbial since there is no constituent to which the numerals are joined. (All the other uses are clearly conjunctive, with καί functioning as a marker of addition.)

Liddell and Scott mention nothing about the etymology of καί. Apparently it is uncertain. Denniston agrees (1954:289–93).

To Denniston the one thing that is certain is that καί marks addition: "its [καί's] primary force is, beyond all reasonable doubt, addition" (p. 289), being evident both with the adverbial and with the conjunctive καί.

Denniston notes further that a series of words are normally either connected by καί throughout or are not connected at all (asyndeton) (for examples see sec. 6.4.3). When connected, prepositions and determiners are ellipsed.[3] Occasionally only the last two constituents are connected. This is the case when they are on a different level from the rest either because of prominence or because of an "et cetera". Denniston also notes that appositionally related items are occasionally linked by καί and that sometimes καί is used where the context implies adversativity or subordination.

---

[2] I understand the first καί as adverbial and the second as conjunctive (see section 4 of chapter 5).

[3] Ellipsis is the omission of words of minor importance to the logical expression of the thought, but necessary to the construction (Smyth 1956:677–78).

CONJUNCTIVE Καί AS A MARKER OF ADDITION 73

In summary, then, the Classical Greek scholars see the basic function of καί as addition (Denniston 1954:289). This is true of the adverbial as well as conjunctive καί.

6.2. How traditional scholars of New Testament Greek view καί

Of all the particles in the New Testament, the conjunctive καί is found the most frequent one by far; it is used 9,164 times. It is used more frequently in the New Testament than in literary Greek, but often in different circumstances. This is one of the things that contributes greatly to the distinctive coloring of the New Testament style. Even so, καί in the New Testament, functions primarily as a connective conjunction translated 'and', just as in Classical Greek. It conjoins formally equal and unequal constituents (e.g., in 1 Tim. 1:10). In the correlative καί ... καί, it is the second particle that functions as a marker of addition. BAGD describe some of its uses as pleonastic.

BAGD (1979:391-93) give the primary function of the connective καί 'and' as follows: It serves to connect *single words* (Rom. 7:12b: the command holy καί just καί good), and it adds the whole to the part, 'and in general' (Acts 5:29: Peter καί the rest of the apostles). Two constituents united by καί can be treated as one expression (Acts 23:6: hope καί [of] resurrection).

The second function of καί, according to BAGD, is to connect *clauses and sentences* (Acts 5:21: and were teaching; καί they sent into prison). Often it is explicative; that is, a word or clause is connected by means of καί with another word or clause for the purpose of explaining what goes before it. When used this way, it is glossed 'and so, that is, namely' (Rom. 1:5: grace, καί, the office of an apostle).

After πολύς and before a second adjective καί is pleonastic from the viewpoint of European languages (John 20:30: many [καί] other signs). This usage is classical (Denniston 1954:290).

The correlative καί ... καί, meaning 'both ... and' or 'not only ... but also' connects single expressions and also whole clauses and sentences (1 Thess. 2:18: καί once καί twice; 1 Cor. 1:22: since καί Jews ask for signs καί Greeks seek wisdom).

Moulton and Turner (1963:343-35) note that καί can sometimes be translated 'and yet' (Matt. 3:14: καί you come to me?) and introduce matters consecutive and final (2 Cor. 11:9: I kept καί I will keep; Matt. 8:21: to return καί to bury my father). They state further that καί may take the place of temporal subordination (Acts 5:12: many wonders happened among the people καί they were in the porch of Solomon). In combination with the future tense καί can resume a purpose clause expressing further result (Matt. 26:53: ask my Father καί he will present).[4] Even though in the New Testament καί sometimes

---

[4] Though popular speech preferred parataxis, as demonstrated by the papyri, in the New Testament the Hebrew ו, which is used to introduce all kinds of subordinate clauses, contributed further to this tendency.

occurs after (καί) ἐγένετο (δέ) instead of an accusative plus infinitive which is a Hebraic/Aramaic construction[5] (Acts 5:7: it happened after three hours, καί his wife entered), it still maintains its additive function in that context. It is no different with the καί ἰδού construction, which to Moulton and Turner seems as redundant as the ἐγένετο construction (Acts 1:10: as they looked into the sky, καί ἰδού two men stood beside them).

In summary, traditional New Testament scholars agree that in the New Testament the conjunctive καί functions mainly as a marker of addition. (They also refer to pleonasm.) While some of the constructions involving καί found in the New Testament are not found in Classical Greek, still they involve the conjoining of contiguous constituents, whether formally equal or unequal.

6.3 How discourse linguists view καί in the New Testament

Levinsohn, Buth, Larsen, and Blass in dealing with the conjunctive καί all agree that it has a coordinating function, primarily joining together formally equal propositions, be they words, phrases, clauses, or sentences. They all recognize that it can conjoin formally unequal constituents as well. Its use implies "continuity."

Levinsohn (1977:20) says of καί's coordinating function, "it unites elements of equal value, weight, or standing." In John's Gospel particularly, it ties together information into event complexes as in John 1:29 and 41 and adds concluding events, speeches, or incidents. At points of discontinuity it associates what follows with what precedes and relates background to foreground as in John 1:24–27) (Levinsohn 1992:43).[6] In a 1981 article Levinsohn demonstrates that in Luke and Acts καί ties together developmental units delimited by δέ.

Buth's view (1991:13) is similar to Levinsohn's: καί has a conjunctive function, joining two or more elements of the same level to each other and indicating continuity with the context, "same situation, same subject matter, same subject or participant."

Larsen sees it this way too: καί is basically a conjoining particle (1991:42–43) that coordinates and establishes close connection between words, phrases, clauses, and sentences. While he attributes more than one use to it, all these uses relate to a basic function of conjoining.

---

[5] While New Testament Greek may be "uncultivated Koine," as Moulton and Turner have it, this is in part due to the audience and in part due to Aramaic influence. The Hebrew ו in the apodosis is frequently rendered by καί in the LXX (cf. Daniel Θ (Theodotian text) 4:2; Matt. 6:4, καί your Father will reward you). In its own way, it is no less interesting and challenging to understand than any other language.

[6] Robson (1980, vol.1, p. 72) claims that in the configuration article-καί-participle, the particle in question is a parenthetical καί: "It adds important information, but not information demanded by the particular context" (Matt. 10:4: Judas Iscariot, the καί having handed him over). What should follow after 'Judas Iscariot' is the parenthesis 'the one who betrayed him' (2 Cor. 1:22; Col. 1:18; 1 Thess. 4:8). But it clearly has the position of an adverbial καί and functions as such.

Titrud (1991:12) also refers to the word-, phrase-, and clause-conjoining function of καί, even though some of its relationships may sometimes involve apposition (1 Cor. 16:16: co-worker καί hard worker) or specification (Phil. 4:6: in every prayer καί intercession).

As to pleonasm, Titrud (1986) points out that all elements of a language are meaningful. "All writers or speakers have reasons for choosing the words which they do, and even unconscious choices are determined by the rules of grammar and style which the writer or speaker has assimilated from childhood" (p. 30). When scholars conclude that pleonasm, or any other anomaly, exists in a language, they are imposing an alien frame of reference onto a particular language; and while the meaning of two particles from two different languages may overlap, this overlap is never total.

According to Titrud, while at times καί encodes a distinction between items it conjoins, at other times it may "express such a close relationship between the conjoined ... propositions that they are often perceived as a single entity" ((1991:10). New Testament authors often mark an appositive by καί in order to reiterate, amplify, specify, or summarize the preceding. Apposition can be recognized when terms, phrases, or clauses joined by καί are synonymous, or nearly so: "The correct meaning in individual contexts is usually that which introduces the least new information to the total context" (p. 11). Titrud also claims that when marking apposition καί encodes thematic prominence (1986:58).[7] (Since there are no examples of καί marking an appositive in the pastoral epistles, with the possible exception of 2 Tim. 2:20, I will not deal with this claim here.)

Blass, in her study of the Pauline Epistles (1993:12-13), presents καί as having a double function: (1) a truth-functional conjunctive function and (2) a constraint-on-relevance adverbial function. When καί is used as a truth-functional marker, it joins together two equal propositions. If one proposition is true, the second one conjoined by καί is also true (Rom. 3:21: attested to by the law καί the prophets; Rom. 3:23: all are sinners καί fall short of the glory of God).

We have seen, then, that all linguists cited agree that καί is a conjoining particle, uniting elements of equal value, weight, and standing (Levinsohn 1977), be they words, phrases, clauses, or sentences. Traditional scholars of the New Testament are in agreement with most of these claims.

6.4 The use of the conjunctive καί in the pastoral Epistles

The pastoral epistles examples of conjunctive καί between contiguous words, phrases, clauses, and sentences show that it is a marker of addition. (In

---

[7] Titrud also holds that when καί conjoins formally unequal constituents, such as a subordinate clause and an independent clause (e.g., Mark 8:3), prominence is given to the subordinate clause (1991:16). In the pastoral epistles, however, the effect of conjoining formally unequal constituents with καί is to treat them as though they were equal (as demonstrated in sec. 6.4.2).

the pastoral epistles it does not introduce any paragraphs, though instances are found in other New Testament books—Levinsohn 1992:32.)

6.4.1 The conjunctive καί between formally equal constituents

In this section it will be shown that the conjunctive καί is a marker of addition between contiguous constituents that are formally equal, whether words, phrases, clauses, or sentences.

6.4.1.1 Contiguous words

The example below displays contiguous adjectives conjoined by καί. In Titus 2:12 three adverbs are conjoined: σωφρόνως 'soberly', δικαίως 'uprightly', εὐσεβῶς 'godly'.

Titus 2:1 σωφρόνως **καὶ** δικαίως **καὶ** εὐσεβῶς ζήσωμεν
        soberly   <u>καί</u> uprightly <u>καί</u> godly   we-should-live

'that we should live soberly, uprightly, and godly'

In 1 Tim. 2:2 ἤρεμον '(quiet')' and ἡσύχιον '(peaceful') are conjoined to modify βίον '(life')':

1 Tim. 2:2 ἵνα   ἤρεμον **καὶ** ἡσύχιον βίον διάγωμεν
        so-that quiet   <u>καί</u> peaceful life we-may-lead

        ἐν πάσῃ εὐσεβείᾳ καὶ σεμνότητι.
        in all godliness and reverence

'that we may lead a quiet and peaceable life, godly and respectful in every way.'

In 2 Tim. 4:21 the conjunctive καί conjoins five contiguous constituents, marking addition. This is a list of people who send their greetings to Timothy (see Denniston 1954:289).

2 Tim. 4:21 Σπούδασον πρὸ χειμῶνος ἐλθεῖν.
        hurry   before winter   to-come

        Ἀσπάζεταί σε   Εὔβουλος
        greets   you Eubulus

        καὶ Πούδης **καὶ** Λίνος **καὶ** Κλαυδία
        <u>καί</u> Pudens <u>καί</u> Linus <u>καί</u> Claudia

        καὶ οἱ ἀδελφοὶ πάντες.
        <u>καί</u> the brothers all

'Do your best to come before winter. Eubulus sends greetings to you, as do Pudens and Linus and Claudia and all the brethren.'

6.4.1.2 Contiguous phrases

In 1 Tim. 1:17 conjunctive καί conjoins two contiguous noun phrases, marking addition:

1 Tim. 1:17a τῷ   δὲ βασιλεῖ τῶν   αἰώνων, ἀφθάρτῳ,
          to-the but king   of-the ages   immortal

ἀοράτῳ,   μόνῳ θεῷ,
invisible only God

'To the King of ages, immortal, invisible, the only God,'

17b τιμὴ **καὶ** δόξα εἰς τοὺς αἰῶνας τῶν   αἰώνων· ἀμήν.
    honor **καί** glory for the   ages   of-the ages   amen

'be honor and glory for ever and ever. Amen.'

In Titus 3:4 conjunctive καί marks an addition between two contiguous complex noun phrases and conjoins them to the genitive τοῦ σωτῆρος ἡμῶν θεοῦ 'of our Savior God'. Though each of these noun phrases has its own article, they are still joined together so closely that the verb is in the singular, signaling that they function as one noun phrase.

Titus 3:4 ὅτε δὲ ἡ χρηστότης **καὶ** ἡ φιλανθρωπία
          when but the kindness   **καί** the love-of-people

ἐπεφάνη   τοῦ   σωτῆρος ἡμῶν θεοῦ,
appeared of-the savior of-our God

'but when the goodness and loving kindness of God our Savior appeared,'

6.4.1.3 Contiguous clauses

In the following examples the conjunctive καί conjoins contiguous clauses, marking addition. The clauses so conjoined may be complement clauses, relative clauses, purpose clauses, conditional clauses, or main clauses. Of the seven examples with conjoined clauses in the pastoral epistles, four contain subordinate clauses. The last three, which are at the end of this section, contain conjoined "main" clauses in the pastoral epistles.

Titus 3:11 εἰδὼς   ὅτι ἐξέστραπται   ὁ   τοιοῦτος
           knowing that has-been-perverted   the such

καὶ ἁμαρτάνει, ὢν   αὐτοκατάκριτος.
καί sins   being   self-condemned

'knowing that such a person is perverted and sinful; he is self-condemned.'

In Titus 3:11 the conjoined clauses are both part of the complement of εἰδὼς and are introduced by ὅτι 'that'.

1 Tim. 6:10 ἡ   φιλαργυρία,   ἧς   τινες ὀρεγόμενοι
            the love-of-money of-which some longing

ἀπεπλανήθησαν ἀπὸ τῆς πίστεως
have-gone-astray from the faith

καὶ ἑαυτοὺς περιέπειραν ὀδύναις πολλαῖς.
καὶ themselves pierced-through with-pangs many

'the love of money . . . it is through this craving that some have wandered away from the faith and pierced their hearts with many pangs.'

In 1 Tim. 6:10 the two contiguous clauses conjoined by καί are introduced by the relative pronoun ἧς 'of which'. Together they function as the compound predicate of τινες.

Titus 2:14 ὃς ἔδωκεν ἑαυτὸν ὑπὲρ ἡμῶν
who gave himself on-behalf of-us

ἵνα λυτρώσηται ἡμᾶς ἀπὸ πάσης ἀνομίας
so-that he-might-redeem us from every lawlessness

καὶ καθαρίσῃ ἑαυτῷ λαὸν περιούσιον
καὶ cleanse for.himself people chosen

'who gave himself for us to redeem us from all iniquity and to purify for himself a people of his own'

In Titus 2:14 the conjunctive καί conjoins two purpose clauses, marking addition and associating them together following ἵνα 'so that'.

1 Tim. 6:3 εἴ τις ἑτεροδιδασκαλεῖ
if someone teaches-differently

καὶ μὴ προσέρχεται ὑγιαίνουσιν λόγοις
καὶ not holds-to sound words

'if anyone teaches otherwise and does not agree with the sound words'

In 1 Tim. 6:3 the conjunctive καί conjoins two conditional clauses marking addition and associating them together following the conditional conjunction εἴ 'if'.

In 1 Tim. 4:11 we can see that conjunctive καί also functions as a marker of addition between *main* clauses:

1 Tim. 4:11 παράγγελε ταῦτα **καὶ** δίδασκε.
command these **καὶ** teach

'Command and teach these things.'

In Titus 2:15 conjunctive καί functions as a marker of addition between *three* contiguous clauses, which are main clauses:

Titus 2:15 Ταῦτα λάλει **καὶ** παρακάλει
these speak **καὶ** encourage

καὶ ἔλεγχε μετὰ πάσης ἐπιταγῆς·
καί reprove with all command

'Declare these things; exhort and reprove with all authority.'

In 2 Tim. 4:17 there is the conjunctive καί which occur three times. The first καί and the third conjoin main clauses; the second joins two purpose clauses. In all of these instances conjunctive καί functions as a marker of addition between contiguous clauses, whether they be subordinate or main.

2 Tim. 4:17 ὁ δὲ κύριός μοι παρέστη
the but Lord me stood-by

καὶ ἐνεδυνάμωσέν με, ἵνα δι' ἐμοῦ
καί empowered me so-that through me

τὸ κήρυγμα πληροφορηθῇ
the proclamation might-be-accomplished

καὶ ἀκούσωσιν πάντα τὰ ἔθνη,
καί might-hear all the nations

καὶ ἐρρύσθην ἐκ στόματος λέοντος.
καί I-was-rescued from mouth of-lion

'But the Lord stood by me and gave me strength to proclaim the message fully, that all the Gentiles might hear it. So I was rescued from the lion's mouth.'

6.4.1.4 Contiguous sentences

The conjunctive καί in some cases conjoins contiguous sentences, marking addition.

1 Tim. 2:13 Ἀδὰμ γὰρ πρῶτος ἐπλάσθη, εἶτα Εὕα·
Adam for first was-created then Eve;

καὶ Ἀδὰμ οὐκ ἠπατήθη,
καί Adam not was-deceived

ἡ δὲ γυνὴ ἐξαπατηθεῖσα ἐν παραβάσει γέγονεν.
the but woman having-been-deceived in transgression was

'For Adam was formed first, then Eve; and Adam was not deceived, but the woman was deceived and became a transgressor.'

In 1 Tim. 2:13 two sentences are introduced by γάρ, showing that they are background information. They provide biblical evidence for Paul's directive to Timothy regarding the activity of women. This explanation is made up of two sentences conjoined by καί, both dealing with Adam and Eve.

1 Tim. 5:16 εἴ τις πιστὴ ἔχει χήρας, ἐπαρκείτω αὐταῖς,
if someone believing has widows let-her-help them

καὶ μὴ βαρείσθω ἡ ἐκκλησία,
__καί__ not let-be-burdened the church

ἵνα ταῖς ὄντως χήραις ἐπαρκέσῃ.
so-that the truly widows it-can-help

'If any believing woman has relatives who are widows, let her assist them; let the church not be burdened, so that it may assist those who are real widows.'

In 1 Tim. 5:16 the conjunctive καί conjoins two contiguous imperative sentences, marking addition. Both sentences deal with responsibility for the welfare of widows in the church.

In Titus 3:9 the function of the conjunctive καί is the same as in the preceding example except the list is of common nouns:

Titus 3:9 μωρὰς δὲ ζητήσεις **καὶ** γενεαλογίας
foolish but arguments __καί__ genealogies

καὶ ἔρεις καὶ μάχας νομικὰς περιΐστασο
__καί__ strife __καί__ battles legal avoid

'But avoid stupid controversies, genealogies, dissensions, and quarrels over the law'

6.4.2 The conjunctive καί between formally unequal constituents

Not only does the conjunctive καί conjoin formally equal constituents, but unequal as well, similarly marking addition. In effect, it is treating them as equal. The following are some examples of this usage.

1 Tim. 2:1 παρακαλῶ οὖν πρῶτον πάντων ποιεῖσθαι δεήσεις...
I-encourage therefore first of-all to-make intercessions

'First of all then, I urge that supplications be made...'

2a ὑπὲρ βασιλέων **καὶ** πάντων τῶν ἐν ὑπεροχῇ ὄντων
for kings __καί__ all the in prominence being

'for kings and all who are in high positions'

Note that in 1 Tim. 1:10 the conjoined constituents are different grammatically: βασιλέων 'kings' is a noun phrase, and πάντων τῶν ἐν ὑπεροχῇ ὄντων 'all those in prominent positions' is a participial phrase with an adjective as its head. But functionally they are equivalent.

The clearest instance of the conjunctive καί functioning as a marker of addition between two formally unequal constituents is in 1 Tim. 1:10, where it is used here to introduce an *et cetera* (Denniston 1954:290) expressed in the form of a conditional clause:

CONJUNCTIVE Καί AS A MARKER OF ADDITION 81

1 Tim. 1:10 πόρνοις,   ἀρσενοκοίταις,
            sexually-immoral homosexuals-with-boys

ἀνδραποδισταῖς, ψεύσταις, ἐπιόρκοις,
slave-traders   liars   perjurers

καί εἴ τι   ἕτερον τῇ διδασκαλίᾳ ἀντίκειται,
καί if something other the teaching opposes

'immoral persons, sodomites, kidnappers, liars, perjurers, and whatever else is contrary to sound doctrine,'

In 2 Tim. 4:1 the conjunctive καί, as a marker of addition, joins a prepositional phrase and an accusative noun phrase:

2 Tim. 4:1 Διαμαρτύρομαι ἐνώπιον τοῦ θεοῦ καὶ Χριστοῦ Ἰησοῦ,
           I-charge   before   the God and Christ Jesus

τοῦ μέλλοντος κρίνειν ζῶντας καὶ νεκρούς,
the intending to-judge living and dead

καὶ τὴν ἐπιφάνειαν αὐτοῦ καὶ τὴν βασιλείαν αὐτοῦ·
καί the appearance of-him and the kingdom   of.him

'I charge you in the presence of God and of Christ Jesus who is to judge the living and the dead, and by his appearing and his kingdom;'

BAGD (1979:186) translate 2 Tim. 4:1 as "I charge you before God and Jesus Christ, and by his appearing." While the constituents are formally different, both relate to διαμαρτύρομαι 'I charge'[8] and are conjoined quite appropriately by conjunctive καί.

In 2 Tim. 3:14 καί functions as a marker of addition between two contiguous constituents, one of which is a relative clause and the other a complement clause, both of which are related to εἰδώς 'knowing'. As in the other examples of this section, the conjunctive καί here conjoins two formally unequal constituents.

2 Tim. 3:14 σὺ δὲ μένε   ἐν οἷς ἔμαθες   καὶ
            you but remain in what you-learned and

ἐπιστώθης   εἰδὼς   παρὰ τίνων ἔμαθες,
became-certain knowing from whom you-learned

'But as for you, continue in what you have learned and have firmly believed, knowing from whom you learned it'

15 καὶ ὅτι ἀπὸ βρέφος [τὰ] ἱερὰ γράμματα οἶδας
   καί that from infancy the holy writings you-know

---

[8] Verbs of swearing take the accusative of the external object (Smyth 1956:359), unless they are followed by a prepositional phrase as in the first part of this text.

'and how from childhood you have been acquainted with the sacred writings'

6.4.3 Καί in relation to the ellipsis of prepositions and determiners

In the pastoral epistles when καί is used to conjoin constituents in the first of which there is a preposition, the preposition is not repeated in the second constituent. This is often true of determiners too. But both prepositions and determiners are repeated when the constituents are juxtaposed without καί. It is my view that the omission of καί constrains the reader to treat the constituents individually, rather than as a conjoined whole.

6.4.3.1 Omission of prepositions when καί conjoins prepositional phrases

In 1 Tim. 4:12 there is an example of conjoined prepositional phrases where the conjunctive καί is absent:

1 Tim. 4:12 μηδείς σου   τῆς νεότητος καταφρονείτω,
no-one of-you the youth   let-despise

ἀλλὰ τύπος γίνου τῶν   πιστῶν   ἐν λόγῳ,
but example be   of-the believers ἐν word

ἐν ἀναστροφῇ, ἐν ἀγάπῃ, ἐν πίστει, ἐν ἁγνείᾳ.
ἐν conduct   ἐν love   ἐν faith   ἐν chastity

'Let no one despise your youth, but set the believers an example in speech and conduct, in love, in faith, in purity.'

When the conjunctive καί is not present, as in the case in 1 Tim. 4:12, the preposition is repeated with every constituent in the same case. Here this emphasizes to Timothy that he is to be an example to the believers in each individual area. Most authorities mentioned by Graham (1976:229) separate with commas the "five spheres" in which Timothy is called to be a model.

In the next two examples the conjunctive καί is *present*, in contrast to the previous example:

1 Tim. 1:5a τὸ δὲ τέλος τῆς   παραγγελίας ἐστὶν ἀγάπη
the but end of-the command   is   love

'whereas the aim of our charge is love'

5b ἐκ καθαρᾶς καρδίας
ἐκ pure   heart

καὶ συνειδήσεως ἀγαθῆς
καί conscience   good

καὶ πίστεως ἀνυποκρίτου,
καί faith   unpretended

'that issues from a pure heart from a good conscience and from sincere faith.'

In 1 Tim. 1:5 all three noun phrases are in the genitive case, the first one being governed by a preposition which requires this case. In the second and third noun phrases, the preposition is omitted; the conjunctive καί precedes these phrases. The three constituents, conjoined with a καί[9] are not individualized, as in 1 Tim. 4:12.

The following is another example in which constituents are conjoined with καί, there being no reason to individualize them:

1 Tim. 2:15a σωθήσεται   δὲ διὰ   τῆς τεκνογονίας,
         she-will-be-saved but through   the childbearing
         'will be saved through bearing children,'

15b ἐὰν μείνωσιν   ἐν πίστει
    if they-remain ἐν faith

    καὶ ἀγάπῃ
    καὶ love

    καὶ ἁγιασμῷ   μετὰ σωφροσύνης.
    καὶ sanctification with self-control

    'if they continue[10] in faith and love and holiness, with modesty.'

6.4.3.2 Omission of determiners when καί conjoins noun phrases

Determiners are repeated, and καί *not* employed, when conjoined constituents are to be treated as individual entities. This can be seen when the author uses more coding material. The more it is used, the more discontinuous the constituents are (Levinsohn 1992:116), as in 2 Tim. 3:10:

2 Tim. 3:10 Σὺ δὲ παρηκολούθησάς   μου τῇ διδασκαλίᾳ,
            you but have-followed-closely of-me τῇ teaching

            τῇ ἀγωγῇ,   τῇ προθέσει, τῇ πίστει,
            τῇ struggle τῇ purpose   τῇ faith

            τῇ μακροθυμίᾳ, τῇ ἀγάπῃ, τῇ ὑπομονῇ,
            τῇ patience   τῇ love   τῇ endurance

            'Now you have observed my teaching, my conduct, my aim in life, my faith, my patience, my love, my steadfastness'

---

[9] The pastoral epistles exhibits no instances in which the preposition is repeated when καί is present. In the New Testament are two such instances when καί appears twice; in ten instances καί appears once (acCordance 1994).

[10] I have amended the RSV text to conform to the GNT text (see RSV footnote).

The repetition of the determiner in 2 Tim. 3:10 indicates that Timothy has followed Paul in each of these individual areas. Guthrie (1957) says, "In a catalogue of nine features the apostle cites his own example...."

In contrast to the preceding example, καί may be present to conjoin constituents and determiners not repeated. This is the case in the pastoral epistles when the constituents are viewed as overlapping. (The determiners are not repeated *unless* the grammar requires it, as in 1 Tim. 6:1.) An example is in 1 Tim. 6:20.

1 Tim. 6:20 Ὦ Τιμόθεε, τὴν παραθήκην φύλαξον,
     oh Timothy the deposit   guard

    ἐκτρεπόμενος   τὰς βεβήλους κενοφωνίας
    turning-away-from <u>τὰς</u> profane chatter

    καὶ ἀντιθέσεις τῆς ψευδωνύμου γνώσεως,
    <u>καί</u> contradiction of-the pseudonymous knowledge

'O Timothy, guard what has been entrusted to you. Avoid the godless chatter; and contradictions of what is falsely called knowledge.'

In 1 Tim. 6:20 καί conjoins κενοφωνίας 'chatter' and ἀντιθέσεις 'contradiction'. The determiner is not repeated with ἀντιθέσεις, since the two noun phrases are viewed as overlapping to some degree and are not discrete. Knight (1992:277) appears to support this point of view: "What Timothy is to avoid is also called ἀντιθέσεις ..., 'opposing arguments or ideas', a term that crystallizes what Paul says elsewhere concerning the false teaching and those who are involved in it...."

Another example of determiners being omitted when καί is present is in 1 Tim. 6:15, coupled also with an example of καί's being *absent* and the determiners being repeated.

1 Tim. 6:15 ἣν καιροῖς ἰδίοις δείξει   ὁ μακάριος
     which in-times own he-will-show <u>ὁ</u> blessed

    καὶ μόνος δυνάστης,
    <u>καί</u> only monarch

    ὁ βασιλεὺς τῶν βασιλευόντων
    <u>ὁ</u> king   of-the kings

    καὶ κύριος τῶν κυριευόντων,
    <u>καί</u> lord of-the lords

'and this will be made manifest at the proper time by the blessed and only Sovereign, the King of kings and the Lord of lords,

16a ὁ μόνος ἔχων ἀθανασίαν,
   <u>ὁ</u> only having immortality

'who alone has immortality'

In the phrases 'blessed and only Sovereign', 'King of kings and Lord of lords', and 'only one who has immortality', the repetition of determiners and the absence of καί indicate that these attributes are each individually ascribed to 'our Lord Jesus Christ' (explicitly mentioned in v. 14). Knight (1992:269) sees these three designations as separate and distinct elements. In contrast, the absence of the determiner and the presence of καί between the two noun phrases in 'King of kings and Lord of lords' signals that they are closely associated and overlap.

While determiners need not be repeated when two or more overlapping constituents are conjoined by καί, they *are* repeated when the grammar requires it because of gender difference, as in 1 Tim. 6:1:

1 Tim. 6:1 Ὅσοι   εἰσὶν ὑπὸ   ζυγὸν δοῦλοι,
          as-many-as   are   under yoke slaves

τοὺς ἰδίους   δεσπότας πάσης τιμῆς ἀξίους ἡγείσθωσαν,
the personal masters all   honor worthy let-them-consider

ἵνα   μὴ τὸ ὄνομα τοῦ   θεοῦ καὶ ἡ διδασκαλία
so-that not τό name of-the God καὶ ἡ teaching

βλασφημῆται.
may-be-blasphemed

'Let all who are under the yoke of slavery regard their masters as worthy of all honor, so that the name of God and the teaching may not be defamed.'

In 1 Tim. 6:1 καί conjoins two contiguous noun phrases, but their genders is different. (They function as the compound subject to βλασφημῆται 'may be blasphemed'.) As far as I can see, the author had no choice but to conjoin the noun phrases with an explicit καί, since the verb is in the singular.

The determiners may also be repeated, even in the presence of καί, for emphasis on different aspects of the overlapping constituents as in 1 Tim. 5:5 and Tit. 3:4. Titrud (1986:64) states, "If two substantives are connected by καί and both have the article, they refer to different persons or things.... If they refer to the same person or thing, different aspects of that which is being described are being accented."

1 Tim. 5:5 ἡ   δὲ ὄντως χήρα καὶ μεμονωμένη
           the but truly widow and remaining

ἤλπικεν   ἐπὶ θεὸν καὶ προσμένει
has-hoped upon God and attends-to

ταῖς δεήσεσιν   καὶ ταῖς προσευχαῖς νυκτὸς   καὶ ἡμέρας·
ταῖς intercessions καὶ ταῖς prayers   of-night and of-day

'She who is a real widow, and is left all alone, has set her hope on God and continues in supplications and prayers night and day'

Note that ταῖς δεήσεσιν 'intercessions' and ταῖς προσευχαῖς 'prayers' are nearly identical in meaning (Knight 1992:219). Paul, in this situation, could have used the second determiner or not. The fact that he used it after καί appears to be significant. He apparently wanted to emphasize the difference between these two kinds of overlapping activities.

Titus 3:4   ὅτε   δὲ   ἡ   χρηστότης   **καὶ** ἡ   φιλανθρωπία
          when   but   ἡ   kindness   <u>καὶ</u> ἡ   love-for-mankind

          ἐπεφάνη   τοῦ   σωτῆρος   ἡμῶν   θεοῦ,
          appeared   of-the   savior   of-us   God

          'but when the goodness and [the] loving kindness of God our Savior appeared'

The Titus 3:4 text is very similar to 1 Tim. 5:5. Knight (1992:338) notes that "the singular ἐπεφάνη appears to indicate that the two terms are considered as one...." On the other hand, the repetition of the determiner implies that the potentially overlapping attributes were viewed as different from each other.

As the examples of sections 6.4.3.1 and 6.4.3.2 show, we can now conclude that the repetition of a preposition or determiner along with the absence of καί indicates that the conjoined constituents are being treated individually, as discrete entities; but when the prepositions or determiners are omitted and καί *is* present, that is an indication that the constituents are being treated as one. Although there are exceptions, as we saw, to this rule of thumb, for reasons of gender difference and emphasis, generally we can say that repetition of the preposition or determiner *separates* the constituents to which they relate whereas their ellipsis brings the constituents *closer*.

6.4.4 The correlative καί ... καί

According to Denniston (1954:323) and Titrud (1991), in a correlative καί ... καί construction the first καί is adverbial, the second conjunctive. Usually they are glossed 'both ... and'. The adverbial καί constrains both constituents to parallel processing (see sec. 5.4.6).

Titus 1:15c   ἀλλὰ μεμίανται αὐτῶν **καὶ** ὁ   νοῦς **καὶ** ἡ   συνείδησις.
           but   defiled   their   <u>καὶ</u> the   mind   <u>καὶ</u> the   conscience

           'their very minds and consciences are corrupted.'

In Titus 1:15c the conjunctive καί functions as a marker of addition between two contiguous noun phrases. The adverbial καί preceding ὁ νοῦς marks this noun phrase for parallel processing with ἡ συνείδησις.

In Titus 1:9b the conjunctive καί likewise marks addition, and the adverbial καί constrains the two contiguous infinitival phrases for parallel processing.

Titus 1:9b   ἵνα   δυνατὸς   ᾖ   **καὶ** παρακαλεῖν
          so-that   able   he-may-be   <u>καὶ</u> to-encourage

ἐν τῇ διδασκαλίᾳ τῇ ὑγιαινούσῃ
in the teaching   the sound

καὶ τοὺς ἀντιλέγοντας ἐλέγχειν.
καὶ the opponents   to-reprove

'so that he may be able to give instruction in sound doctrine and also confute those who contradict it.'

In the next example, the conjoined phrases are not contiguous:

1 Tim. 4:16 γὰρ ποιῶν **καὶ** σεαυτὸν σώσεις   **καὶ** τοὺς ἀκούοντάς σου.
for doing **καὶ** yourself you-will-save   **καὶ** the hearing   you

'for by so doing you will save both yourself and your hearers.'

Here the conjunctive καί conjoins two noun phrases: σεαυτὸν 'yourself' and τοὺς ἀκούοντάς σου 'those who hear you'. As Levinsohn (1992:90) points out, "Complex rhematic constituents are discontinuous, with one part preceding the verb and the other part occurring after...." In this instance the "complex rhematic constituent" is the correlative 'both yourself and your hearers', with the adverbial καί constraining the two constituents to parallel processing, just as in the previously cited examples.

6.5 Occurrences of καί that could be either adverbial or conjunctive

Some occurrences of καί could be interpreted as either adverbial or conjunctive. I deal here first with those that I consider to be adverbial and then with those that I consider to be conjunctive.

1 Tim. 5:6 ἡ δὲ σπαταλῶσα ζῶσα τέθνηκεν.
the but luxuriously living is-dead

'whereas she who is self-indulgent is dead even while she lives.'

7 **καὶ** ταῦτα παράγγελλε, ἵνα ἀνεπίλημπτοι ὦσιν.
καὶ these command   so-that blameless   they-may-be

'Command this, so that they may be without reproach.'

In 1 Tim. 5:7 καί does not *conjoin* the v. 7 sentence to the one in v. 6, since v. 6 is concerned with a widow living luxuriously and v. 7, as ταῦτα 'these things' indicates, with *all* that Paul said in vv. 3–6. (The command is addressed to the children and grandchildren of v. 4 [Knight 1992:220]). Rather it is an *adverbial* καί here, constraining the clause introduced by it (v. 7) to parallel processing with 1 Tim. 4:11: παράγγελλε ταῦτα καὶ δίδασκε 'command these and teach'.

In 2 Tim. 3:5 again there is a question whether καί is adverbial or conjunctive:

2 Tim. 3:5a ἔχοντες μόρφωσιν εὐσεβείας
having form   of-godliness

τὴν δὲ δύναμιν αὐτῆς ἠρνεμένοι·
the but power of-it denying

'holding the form of religion but denying the power of it.'

5b καὶ τούτους ἀποτρέπου.
καί these avoid

'Avoid such people.'

The 2 Tim. 3:5 context appears to point to adverbial καί. For one thing, imperatives in the pastoral epistles are not usually preceded by καί unless conjoined to another imperative as in 2 Tim. 1:8, 13, 14, etc. (An exception is in 2 Tim. 2:19.) For this reason Knight (1992:433) proposes that καί conjoins the imperative in this verse with the imperative in 3:1. This is unlikely, since the two imperatives are not contiguous. Furthermore, his proposal does not take account of the explanatory γάρ in v. 2. Viewed as an adverbial, however, the presence of καί makes sense: in addition to other people that Timothy ('you') has already been instructed to avoid,[11] he is to avoid these *also* (καί).

The καί in 2 Tim. 3:11b is another one open to question:

2 Tim. 3:10 Σὺ δὲ παρηκολούθησάς μου τῇ διδασκαλίᾳ,
you but have-followed-closely of-me the teaching

τῇ ἀγωγῇ, τῇ προθέσει, τῇ πίστει, τῇ μακροθυμίᾳ,
the struggle the purpose the faith the patience

τῇ ἀγωγῇ, τῇ ὑπομονῇ,
the love the endurance

'Now you have observed my teaching, my conduct, my aim in life, my faith, my patience, my love, my steadfastness,'

11a τοῖς διωγμοῖς, τοῖς παθήμασιν,
the persecutions the sufferings

οἷά μοι ἐγένετο ἐν Ἀντιοχείᾳ, ἐν Ἰκονίῳ,
which to-me happened in Antioch in Iconium

11b ἐν Λύστροις, οἵους διωγμοὺς ὑπήνεγκα·
in Lystra which persecutions I-endured

11c καὶ ἐκ πάντων με ἐρρύσατο ὁ κύριος.
καί out of-all me delivered the Lord

'my persecutions, my sufferings, what befell me at Antioch, at Iconium, and at Lystra, what persecutions I endured; yet from them all the Lord rescued me.'

---

[11] The 'other people' are implied but may be similar to or identical with those whom Paul mentions in chapter 2:16–18.

The 11c clause introduced by καί cannot readily be conjoined with the one in v. 10 (σὺ δὲ παρηκολούθησάς μου διδασκαλίᾳ, etc., since the phrase ἐκ πάντων 'out of all-things' does not refer to all the items enumerated in v. 10. This phrase together with ἐρρύσατο obviously pertains to τοῖς διωγμοῖς and τοῖς παθήμασιν in 11a. Travis (1972:147) suggests that this καί is conjunctive, glossing it 'yet'; he says it is ascensive in force. Knight agrees. He states, "Paul adds a note of triumph in the Lord that marks his accounts of suffering and persecution..." (1992:440).

In 2 Tim. 2:20 καί is conjunctive, in my view:

2 Tim. 2:20a Ἐν μεγάλῃ δὲ οἰκίᾳ οὐκ ἔστιν
           in great but house not is

           μόνον σκεύη χρυσᾶ καὶ ἀργυρᾶ
           only vessels golden and silver

           ἀλλὰ καὶ ξύλινα καὶ ὀστράκινα,
           but also wooden and earthen

'In a great house there are not only vessels of gold and silver but also of wood and earthenware,'

20b **καὶ** ἃ μὲν εἰς τιμὴν ἃ δὲ εἰς ἀτιμίαν·
     <u>καί</u> what on-the-one-hand for honor what but for dishonor

'and some for noble use, some for ignoble.'

Here the conjunctive καί is marking addition between two contiguous main clauses. Minor (1992:79) translates this καί as 'and' but without further note. Knight (1992:417–18) suggests that it might function "explicatively," translating it 'that is, namely', "indicating that the phrase that follows is intended to explain what went before" (see also BAGD 1979:393). However, καί does not indicate apposition here; it functions in a conjunctive sense and marks addition.[12]

The final example of καί that is open to question is in 1 Tim. 3:16; I take it to be conjunctive:

1 Tim. 3:15b ἥτις ἐστὶν ἐκκλησία θεοῦ ζῶντος,
           which is church of-God living

           στῦλος καὶ ἑδραίωμα τῆς ἀληθείας
           pillar and foundation of-the truth

'which is the church of the living God, the pillar and bulwark of the truth.'

16 **καὶ** ὁμολογουμένως μέγα ἐστὶν
    <u>καί</u> confessedly great is

---

[12] Apposition can also be indicated by asyndeton (1 Tim. 3:15, 6:16; 2 Tim. 3:8; Tit. 2:14).

τὸ τῆς   εὐσεβείας μυστήριον·
the of-the godliness mystery
'Great indeed, we confess, is the mystery of our religion'

Here in v. 15 Paul gives a directive to Timothy about his conduct in the church, the church being the pillar and foundation of the truth. Then in v. 16 he refers to the great confession of the church. At first glance it is difficult to see the connection between the two. Knight (1992:182) writes, "Having ended the last verse with emphasis on the truth of the gospel, Paul now writes of the confessed grandeur of the gospel in terms of him who is its reality." If we take τὸ τῆς εὐσεβείας μυστήριον 'the mystery of godliness' to refer back to τῆς ἀληθείας 'of the truth', καί is conjunctive, functioning as a marker of addition between two contiguous clauses.

6.6 Conclusion

Traditional scholars of Classical Greek and New Testament Greek, as well as discourse linguists, view the basic function of καί, whether adverbial or conjunctive, as additive. This additive function is present whether formally *equal* or formally *unequal* constituents are joined. The pastoral epistles texts confirm this position; in the pastoral epistles the function of καί is always additive, whether it is adverbial or conjunctive. As a conjunction καί conjoins contiguous constituents, be they words, phrases, clauses, or sentences, formally equal or not. It processes the following material as an addition to, not as a development of, what precedes. Only in a correlative construction (see sec. 6.4.4) has καί been found to conjoin noncontiguous constituents.

7 Οὖν As a Marker of Inference

In Classical Greek, οὖν had two orientations. Originally, it was an adverb of affirmation, 'indeed, truly, certainly'. Later, it came to function as a conjunction as well. The two conjunctive uses, inferential and continuative, may be glossed 'therefore' and 'thus' respectively, with the latter affirming an inference drawn from what precedes. In the New Testament the adverbial οὖν does not seem to occur; most likely it was not extant in the time of the New Testament.

Here in chapter 7 my concern is to demonstrate that the basic use of the conjunctive οὖν is the inferential one. The continuative function, which is a weakened use of the inferential, appears primarily in a specific context. The inferential can be described as the "default use" of the conjunctive οὖν; the continuative is the "specialized use." The continuative use is seen only in particular contexts (see sec. 7.4.2); in Luke and John it also occurs after participles (Luke 23:22: having scourged him οὖν, I will release him; John 6:5: upon raising his eyes οὖν, Jesus . . . said).

7.1 How traditional scholars of Classical Greek view οὖν

In Classical Greek, οὖν—like a number of other Greek conjunctions (e.g., ἀλλά, γάρ, and καί)—has a twofold character; it may function as an adverb or a conjunction. As an adverb it is affirmative, 'certainly, indeed'. As a conjunction it may function either in an inferential way, 'then, therefore' or in a continuative way, 'so, then, thus'.

Schwyzer and Debrunner (1950, vol. 2, pp. 584–85) note that οὖν was originally an affirmative adverb, glossed 'indeed, truly, certainly' (an example is in Thucydides III.45,1), and in the fifth century B.C. authors started using it as a conjunction, either continuative (Herodotus I.36) or inferential. In Koine Greek, according to Schwyzer and Debrunner, only the conjunctive function survives.

KG (1955, vol. 2, pp. 155, 326) hold the same view as Schwyzer and Debrunner regarding the original function of οὖν. Regarding the syllogistic[1] (i.e., inferential) and continuative uses of the conjunctive οὖν, they say it came to mean 'thus' or 'therefore' and affirmed an inference drawn from the preceding proposition: "by it [the conjunction] the consequences which were drawn

---

[1] Their definition of syllogistic, if I understand it correctly, is different from that of Winer. For the latter, syllogism is "indicative rather of continuation and retrospect than of inference" (Winer 1877:555, fn.4). For the former, it is inferential; for the latter, resumptive.

from that which preceded were expressed as something that really happened"[2] (KG 1955, vol. 2, pp. 326).

According to Liddell and Scott (1940:1272) the particle οὖν[3] in Classical Greek has three major functions. The first is as an adverb, 'certainly, in fact', confirming something, frequently in contrast with something that is not confirmed. In Homer it appears only in combination with γε (as γοῦν), γάρ, οὔτε or μήτε, ὡς, ἐπεί, μέν, etc. (Iliad 2:350: I declare that Zeus did *really* promise). It can also be added to indefinite pronouns and adverbs; for example, ὅστις 'whoever' becomes ὁστισοῦν 'whosoever', and ὅπως 'how' becomes ὁπωσοῦν, 'howsoever'.

The second and third functions described by Liddell and Scott are conjunctive in nature. The second glossed 'so, then' is to continue a narrative (Xenophon's *Cyrus* 4:1.22: Then immediately Cyrus said) or to resume after a parenthesis or a long protasis (Herodotus 1.69). The third function glossed 'then, therefore', appears in inferences. This use is not in Homer and only rarely in Aeschylus, and then usually in questions. It is quite common from Herodotus onwards: καὶ σὺ οὖν 'you too therefore' (Xenophon's *Cyrus*, 4:1.20); it can be strengthened by the addition of δή (as in Plato's *Symposium* 191c). It also appears in questions (Aeschylus's *Prometheus Vinctus*, 771: Who οὖν is the one that set you free?).

Smyth (1956:664) writes that οὖν is either confirmatory (as an adverb), glossed 'in fact, at all events, in truth', or inferential (as a conjunction), glossed 'therefore, accordingly', signifying that something follows from what precedes. It "points to something already mentioned or known or to the present situation."

Schwyzer and Debrunner, KG, Liddell and Scott, and Smyth thus agree that in Classical Greek οὖν functions as a confirmatory adverb, meaning 'certainly', and as a continuative conjunction, 'so, then', and as an inferential conjunction, 'then, therefore'. While the original function was adverbial, the function as a conjunction with a dual use derived from this particular orientation. According to Schwyzer and Debrunner, and Liddell and Scott, the order of development seems to have been first continuative and then inferential. Denniston (1954:416), Smyth, and KG, on the other hand, take the reverse order. The inferential use is more frequent. My analysis of the pastoral epistles leads me to take the inferential to be primary too (see sec. 7.4).

---

[2] My translation of the German, which reads as follows: "Aus der versichernden Bedeutung dieses Adverbs hat sich später der syllogistische Gebrauch von οὖν als Konjunktion ... entwickelt, indem die aus dem Vorhergehenden gezogene Folgerung als eine jedenfalls stattfindende ausgesprochen wird."

[3] Ionic and Doric ὦν (Liddell and Scott 1940:1272).

7.2 How traditional scholars of New Testament Greek view οὖν

Just as the majority of traditional Classical Greek scholars consider conjunctive οὖν to introduce inference, so do the scholars of the New Testament. It is used in nearly all of the New Testament writings, though more frequently in narrative, and most extensively in the Gospel of John (194 times), but rarely in the Johannine epistles and in Revelation. It occurs 493 times in all the New Testament.

In general, New Testament Greek scholars indicate that conjunctive οὖν has two basic functions, causal (i.e., inferential) and temporal (i.e., continuative). Some mention additional uses, such as, adverbial and adversative, but they seem to be rather unlikely.

BDR (1976:381) write that while οὖν is basically causal (i.e., inferential), it is also used to introduce temporal (i.e., continuative) connections, especially in narrative.[4] It continues a narrative or leads back to the main theme. The inferential and continuative functions are especially prominent in John's Gospel (see Moulton and Turner 1963:337-38).

Winer's view is similar (1877:555). He notes that οὖν is the most common particle expressing consequence (i.e., inference) and can also function as a syllogistic (i.e., continuative) particle.[5] In many instances it marks the progress of a narrative (John 4:5: οὖν he came into a city of the Samaritans called Sychar). After a parenthetical clause it takes up the train of thought again (1 Cor. 8:4: Regarding food offered to idols οὖν).

BAGD (1979:592-93) have the most extensive listing of uses of οὖν. They hold that it is an inferential conjunction as well as a continuative conjunction, the latter being its main use. Of four major uses, they list the inferential one first, meaning that what it introduces is the result of or an inference from what precedes. It can be translated 'so, therefore, consequently, accordingly, then', and occurs in statements, commands, invitations, and questions. Examples are in Eph. 4:1 (I encourage you οὖν to live worthily) and Phil. 2:29 (receive him οὖν with all joy).

The second major use of the conjunctive οὖν cited by BAGD is that it may resumes a subject after an interruption in historical narrative. This is glossed 'so, as has been said'. It may also indicate a transition to something new and, used in this way, means 'now, then'. In some places οὖν indicates a response: 'in reply, in return' as in 1 Cor. 11:20 (when you gather οὖν) and John 4:9a (οὖν the Samaritan woman said to him).

BAGD's third use of οὖν, the emphatic, shows traces of classical usage: 'certainly, really, to be sure' as in 1 Cor. 3:5 (what οὖν is Apollos?). However,

---

[4] According to Denniston (1954:425-26), in narrative οὖν is "almost purely temporal, marking a new stage in the sequence of events: 'Well', 'Now'".

[5] In order to explain what he means by this, Winer (1877:555, fn. 4) presents a quotation from "Don" (I could not find information on this name in the book) to the effect that the particle should be rendered 'accordingly, as was said, to proceed', rather than 'therefore', which is expressed by ἄρα and its compounds.

they also give an alternate classification for this reference. The fourth use of οὖν, according to BAGD, is the adversative 'but, however', as in Rom. 10:14 (how οὖν shall they call him in whom they did not believe?).

The inferential, continuative, and emphatic functions are plausible on the basis of their occurrence in Classical Greek. Regarding BAGD's (1979:593.4) "adversative" sense, they present it with an admission of a weak case. And since Classical Greek has no equivalent of this use[6] and BDR (1976:381) make no mention of an adversative function of οὖν, I contend that the adversative understanding of οὖν in John 9:18, Acts 23:21, 25:4, 28:5, and Rom. 10:14 (some of the passages cited by BAGD in support of a possible adversative meaning) is contextually inferred, not a function of the particle itself.[7]

7.3 How discourse linguists view οὖν in the New Testament

Blass (1993:4) begins her discussion of οὖν with the combination ἄρα οὖν. She claims that this collocation marks conclusions regarding matters for which Paul argued in his letters, an example being Rom. 8:12 (ἄρα οὖν, brothers, we are not debtors to the flesh to live according to the flesh) which functions as a conclusion for vv. 1–11. The collocation with ἄρα encourages the assumption that οὖν marks conclusions. However, it is not οὖν that marks the conclusion, but ἄρα, an inferential particle translated 'so, then, consequently' by BAGD (1979:103).

Blass further claims (p. 5) that οὖν by itself can mark a potential conclusion. When it is combined with a rhetorical question, indicated by a following μὴ γένοιτο, as in Rom. 3:3 (do we οὖν set aside the law through faith? μὴ γένοιτο!),[8] it can imply a possible conclusion to be drawn by a reader on the basis of contextual assumptions, some of which Paul comes to reject emphatically. It seems to me, however, that οὖν by itself is not so much conclusive as inferential; it has to be used in connection with a rhetorical question to mark a possible conclusion. At any rate, the preceding examples show that communication is inferential in nature, as Blass herself states (loc. cit.).

Poythress (1984:327–29) claims that in expository contexts οὖν functions to indicate logical inference (reason-result or grounds-implication). He also discusses the continuative use of οὖν, saying that οὖν is the unmarked conjunction of choice to express the resumption of the main line after a digression and also to continue a narrative when the agent shifts while the action stays the

---

[6] Denniston (1954:424, fn. 1) says, "There is no adequate evidence for an adversative οὖν."

[7] Larsen also sees that the adversative use as unlikely (1991:39).

[8] In the Pauline correspondence, particularly in Romans, 1 Corinthians. and Galatians μὴ γένοιτο appears fourteen times ; it marks a preceding question thirteen times (macBible 1988).

same.⁹ In John, he says, οὖν is used to intimate a quasi-causal relationship (p. 329).

Larsen says (1991:38-9), "the basic relationship expressed by οὖν is consequence" by which he means inference. In addition, as in Classical Greek, it signals continuation, he says. He suggests that the eight functions proposed by Moulton and Turner (1976:1104) can be subsumed under inference and continuation.¹⁰ The adversative function (no. 6 of Moulton and Turner) Larsen considers suspect, since there is no connection between it and either inference or continuation.

For the gospel of John in particular, Reimer (1985:35) claims that οὖν functions both on the discourse and the thematic levels. Its discourse function is "that of moving the story line along by introducing 'distinctive information' which furthers the author's purpose." Its thematic function is "that of monitoring the tension of the developing theme according to the author's purpose."¹¹

Levinsohn (1992:44-46) points out that in John οὖν is a specialized developmental conjunction in contexts where other writers would have used δέ (viz. in contexts where the logical relationship with the context is emphasized). Its presence marks a return to the story line after a parenthetical comment (as in John 4:1-7) and a logical relationship to previous material (John 1:39). It also introduces speeches linked by asyndeton (John 4:33-34).

Buth (1992:145, 157) compares the function of οὖν with καί, δέ, and asyndeton in the Gospels and Acts. In doing so he notes that the developmental connector in the Synoptics and Acts is δέ, but that John in his Gospel uses both δέ and οὖν as developmental connectors. Later in Buth's 1992 article, after he has presented these same connectors as a four-celled matrix composed of two parameters, close connection and significant change, he states, "These are pragmatic, structural devices for presenting the continuous flow of sentences and for aiding the reader in processing the information" (p. 157).

As Buth (pp. 147-49) sees it, οὖν marks significant change and close logical connection, introducing significant material. Thus he posits three functions for οὖν in John: (1) to indicate resumption after background material (but thematic development and close connection must be present—see John 6:3-5); (2) to

---

⁹ Buth does not consider this to be a function of οὖν, since other connecting devices indicate change of agent and οὖν can be used with the same agent (see John 4:40). He thinks that something else must be going on here (1992:149-50).

¹⁰ MT's eight functions are (1) inference/logical consequence; (2) consequent command/exhortation; (3) consequent effect or response; (4) inferential questions; (5) summary (a final inference, a conclusive statement); (6) adversative; (7) continuation or resumption of narrative; and (8) continuation of discussion.

¹¹ Larsen (1991:39) expresses doubt about these two hypotheses (see also Levinsohn 1992:44-45). He further claims that tension in John's Gospel should be correlated with the historic present and not with the presence of οὖν.

establish logical/close connection (see John 1:39 and 11:46-47); and (3) to begin new units and event groupings (see John 4:28-34).[12]

In summary, my view is that Blass's claims for οὖν as a conclusion marker are tenable only under very restricted circumstances. Though she calls οὖν a marker of conclusion, a more accurate label is inference. Buth refers to "close logical connection," Poythress "logical inference," and Larsen "consequence." (I consider Poythress and Larsen to be referring to the inferential function of οὖν.) Levinsohn and Buth point out that οὖν also can introduce specialized development. Poythress, Larsen, Levinsohn, and Buth all mention the "resumptive" οὖν which I would classify under continuation. Discourse linguists in general hold that the inferential function of οὖν is primary and the continuative secondary, appearing primarily in narrative.

7.4 The use of οὖν in the pastoral Epistles

In the pastoral epistles οὖν is seen to be primarily a marker of inference and secondarily a marker of continuation, the latter appearing only in resumptive contexts.

7.4.1 The inferential function of οὖν

As the following examples show, οὖν is an introducer of inference when there is no interruption in the argument.

2 Tim. 2:20 Ἐν μεγάλῃ δὲ οἰκίᾳ οὐκ ἔστιν μόνον σκεύη
in great but house not is only vessels

χρυσᾶ καὶ ἀργυρᾶ ἀλλὰ καὶ ξύλινα καὶ ὀστράκινα,
gold and silver but also wood and clay

καὶ ἃ μὲν εἰς τιμὴν ἃ δὲ εἰς ἀτιμίαν·
and some on-the-one-hand for honor some but for dishonor

'In a great house there are not only vessels of gold and silver but also of wood and earthenware, and some for noble use, some for ignoble.'

21 ἐὰν **οὖν** τις ἐκκαθάρῃ ἑαυτὸν ἀπὸ τούτων,
if <u>οὖν</u> someone cleanses himself from these

ἔσται σκεῦος εἰς τιμήν, ἡγιασμένον, εὔχρηστον τῷ
he-will-be vessel for honor set-aside useful for-the

δεσπότῃ, εἰς πᾶν ἔργον ἀγαθὸν ἡτοιμασμένον.
master for every work good prepared

---

[12] Buth notes two other possible functions: (4) background, as a facetious suggestion (οὖν usually suggests that the material following it is *not* background, and only if it can precede non-events, which are background, would it have this function [cf. John 11:54]); and (5) switch subject (i.e., new agent).

'If anyone purifies himself from what is ignoble, then he will be a vessel for noble use, consecrated; and useful to the master of the house, ready for any good work.'

In 2 Tim. 2:20 Paul introduces the analogy of a royal household with a developmental δέ. Its many vessels made from different materials (v. 20) all have their use, whether noble or ignoble. From this analogy Paul draws an inference for each individual Christian introduced by οὖν (v. 21). Whenever a person cleanses himself, he will be a vessel for noble use, serviceable to the Lord and ready for every good work. What ties the analogy and the application together is the phrase εἰς τιμήν 'for honor'. The analogy becomes the ground for Paul's exhortation. According to Knight (1992:418), it "indicates that the statement it introduces is an inference drawn from the last phrase of v. 20: Since some vessels are for honor, one should 'therefore' seek to be one of them." Most other commentators also support the inferential notion here (see Minor 1992:80).

1 Tim. 3:1 Πιστὸς ὁ λόγος· εἴ τις ἐπισκοπῆς ὀρέγεται,
faithful the word if someone oversight reaches-after

καλοῦ ἔργου ἐπιθυμεῖ.
good work he-desires

'This saying is sure: If any one aspires to the office of a bishop, he desires a noble task.'

2 δεῖ οὖν τὸν ἐπίσκοπον ἀνεπίλημπτον
it-is-necessary οὖν the overseer blameless

εἶναι, μιᾶς γυναικὸς ἄνδρα, νηφάλιον,
to-be of-one wife husband sober

σώφρονα, κόσμιον, φιλόξενον, διδακτικόν.
sensible modest love-of-strangers able-to-teach

'Now a bishop must be above reproach, the husband of one wife, temperate, sensible, dignified, hospitable, an apt teacher'

The focus in 1 Tim. 3:1-2 is on oversight in terms of activity (ἐπισκοπή) and actor (ἐπίσκοπος). A person who reaches out after such an office desires a good work. From the fact that oversight is "a good work" Paul concludes that the life of a person who aspires to it will reflect the nature of the office. His life will be beautiful (καλός), corresponding to his office (καλὸν ἔργον). In this context οὖν is most likely inferential. Knight (1992:155) writes, "Οὖν indicates that an inference is to be drawn. δεῖ ... states the inference to be drawn by means of the accusative and infinitive that follow." Most commentators also see οὖν as inferential in this text.

7.4.2 The continuative function of οὖν

When οὖν is continuative in the pastoral epistles it is in a specialized context, namely that of resumption of an earlier topic, seen in 1 Tim. 1:18–2:2.

1 Tim. 1:18 Ταύτην   τὴν παραγγελίαν παρατίθεμαί   σοι,
            this   the command   I-place-before   you

            τέκνον Τιμόθεε, κατὰ   τὰς προαγούσας
            child   Timothy   according-to the coming-before

            ἐπὶ   σὲ   προφητείας, ἵνα   στρατεύῃ
            upon you prophecies   so-that you-may-fight

            ἐν   αὐταῖς τὴν καλὴν στρατείαν,
            with   them   the   good   fight

'This charge I commit to you, Timothy, my son, in accordance with the prophetic utterances which pointed to you, that inspired by them you may wage the good warfare.'

     19 ἔχων   πίστιν καὶ ἀγαθὴν συνείδησιν, ἥν   τινες
        having faith   and   good   conscience   which some

        ἀπωσάμενοι   περὶ   τὴν πίστιν ἐναυάγησαν·
        after-rejecting concerning the faith   made-shipwreck

'holding faith and a good conscience. By rejecting conscience, certain persons have made shipwreck of their faith,'

     20 ὧν   ἐστιν Ὑμέναιος   καὶ Ἀλέξανδρος,
        of-which   is   Hymenaeus and Alexander

        οὓς   παρέδωκα   τῷ   Σατανᾷ ἵνα
        whom   I-handed-over to-the Satan   so-that

        παιδευθῶσιν   μὴ   βλασφημεῖν.
        they-might-be-taught not to-speak-evil

'among them Hymenaeus and Alexander, whom I have delivered to Satan that they may learn not to blaspheme.'

    2:1 Παρακαλῶ **οὖν** πρῶτον πάντων ποιεῖσθαι δεήσεις,
       I-encourage <u>οὖν</u> first   of-all   to-make   intercessions

       προσευχάς, ἐντεύξεις, εὐχαριστίας,
       prayers   entreaties thanksgivings

       ὑπὲρ   πάντων ἀνθρώπων,
       on-behalf-of all   people

'First of all, then, I urge that supplications, prayers, intercessions, and thanksgivings be made for all men,'

οὖν AS A MARKER OF INFERENCE

2 ὑπὲρ   βασιλέων καὶ πάντων τῶν ἐν ὑπεροχῇ ὄντων,
  on-behalf-of kings   and all   the in authority being

  ἵνα   ἤρεμον   καὶ ἡσύχιον βίον
  so-that undisturbed and quiet   life

  διάγωμεν   ἐν πάσῃ εὐσεβείᾳ καὶ σεμνότητι.
  we-may-lead in all godliness and honesty

'for kings and all who are in high positions, that we may lead a quiet and a peaceable life, godly and respectful in every way.'

Paul's first letter to Timothy began with instruction (1:3) to Timothy for his work as a pastor, warning against the incursions of false teachers. Then in vv. 12–17 the topic is God's grace for Paul as a persecutor of the church. In vv. 18–20 Paul urges Timothy to "fight the good fight" and keep a good conscience, in contrast to some who made shipwreck of their faith. Then in 2:1–2 Paul returns to his instruction to Timothy, first urging that Christians pray for those in authority and then going on to other such instructions. It is not apparent that the function of οὖν in this text is inferential. Indeed, nearly all the commentators agree that οὖν in this context is resumptive. For example, Guthrie (1957:69) writes, "The main business of the Epistle now begins and in the opening words of this section Paul appears to continue the theme of i.3." Not only does 2:1 resume the theme of what Timothy is directed to do, but it also develops it by moving to a new point; this is in line with the claim of Levinsohn and Buth for resumptive οὖν (see also BAGD). I therefore conclude that οὖν is indeed continuative in 1 Tim. 2:1.

2 Tim. 1:16 δῴη   ἔλεος ὁ κύριος τῷ   'Ονησιφόρου   οἴκῳ,
            may-give mercy the Lord to-the of-Onesiphorus house

  ὅτι   πολλάκις με ἀνέψυξεν
  because often   me he-refreshed

  καὶ τὴν ἅλυσίν μου   οὐκ ἐπαισχύνθη,
  and the chains of-me not he-was-ashamed

'May the Lord grant mercy to the household of Onesiphorus, for he often refreshed me; he was not ashamed of my chains,'

17 ἀλλὰ γενόμενος   ἐν 'Ρώμῃ
   but upon-coming to Rome

   σπουδαίως ἐζήτησέν με καὶ εὗρεν·
   quickly   he-sought me and found

'but when he arrived in Rome, he searched for me eagerly and found me'

18 δῴη   αὐτῷ ὁ κύριος εὑρεῖν ἔλεος
   may-give to-him the Lord to-find mercy

παρὰ κυρίου ἐν ἐκείνῃ τῇ ἡμέρᾳ.
before Lord   in that   the day

καὶ ὅσα ἐν Ἐφέσῳ διηκόνησεν, βέλτιον σὺ   γινώσκεις.
and what in Ephesus he-served   better yourself you-know

'may the Lord grant him to find mercy from the Lord on the Day—and you well know all the service he rendered at Ephesus.'

2:1 Σὺ **οὖν**, τέκνον μου, ἐνδυναμοῦ
you <u>οὖν</u> child of-me strengthen-yourself

ἐν τῇ χάριτι τῇ ἐν Χριστῷ Ἰησοῦ
with the grace the in Christ Jesus

'You then, my son, be strong in the grace that is in Christ Jesus,'

2 καὶ ἃ   ἤκουσας παρ' ἐμοῦ διὰ
and what you-heard from me   through

πολλῶν μαρτύρων, ταῦτα παράθου πιστοῖς ἀνθρώποις,
many   witnesses these entrust.to faithful men

οἵτινες ἱκανοὶ   ἔσονται καὶ ἑτέρους διδάξαι.
who   sufficient will-be also others   to-teach

'and what you have heard from me before many witnesses entrust to faithful men who will be able to teach others also'

In the larger context of 2 Tim. 1:16–2:2 Paul recalls to Timothy his experience of being bereft of most of his companions (1:15). In vv. 16-18 he goes on to mention Onesiphorus, who had been of such great comfort to him. Thereupon he resumes at 2:1 the giving of directives to the members of the church through Timothy. A few commentators take οὖν to be inferential (see Minor 1992:42),[13] for example, Knight (1992:388). Knight, however, weakens his case somewhat by saying that Paul here "turns to a renewed direct address to Timothy," which appears to imply that the particle is resumptive. Indeed, since 1:15-18 contains no exhortation to Timothy, whereas both 1:13-14 and all of chapter 2 do, it seems very likely that οὖν is *not* inferential, but rather resumptive, returning to Paul's instructions that Timothy is to pass on to the church.

In summary, then, in the pastoral epistles οὖν is continuative only in a context of introducing resumption of an earlier topic. In such a context the inferential idea would not make sense. The resumption, it should be noted, involves development of the topic, which is why Levinsohn (1992:44) calls it, in the Gospel of John, "a specialized developmental conjunction."

---

[13] A considerable number of commentators make no reference at all to the conjunction.

7.4.3 The function of οὖν when the previous context is introduced by γάρ

Even when it is resumptive, οὖν may have inferential force. This is the case if the interruption that preceded it is composed of supportive material introduced by γάρ.

1 Tim. 5:11a νεωτέρας δὲ χήρας παραιτοῦ·
           younger but widows refuse

      11b ὅταν **γὰρ** καταστρηνιάσωσιν τοῦ Χριστοῦ,
           whenever <u>for</u> they-become-wanton-against the Christ

           γαμεῖν θέλουσιν,
           to-marry they-wish

           'But refuse to enroll younger widows; for when they grow wanton against Christ they desire to marry,'

      12 ἔχουσαι κρίμα ὅτι τὴν πρώτην πίστιν ἠθέτησαν·
           having judgment that the first faith they-set-aside

           'and so they incur condemnation, for having violated their first pledge.'

      13 ἅμα δὲ καὶ ἀργαὶ μανθάνουσιν,
           at-the-same-time but also lazy they learn (to be)

           περιερχόμεναι τὰς οἰκίας, οὐ μόνον δὲ ἀργαὶ
           going-about the houses not only but lazy

           ἀλλὰ καὶ φλύαροι καὶ περίεργοι,
           but also babbling and busybodies

           λαλοῦσαι τὰ μὴ δέοντα.
           speaking the not being-necessary

           'Besides that, they learn to be idlers, gadding about from house to house, and not only idlers but gossips and busybodies, saying what they should not.'

      14 βούλομαι **οὖν** νεωτέρας γαμεῖν, τεκνογονεῖν,
           I-want <u>οὖν</u> younger-ones to-marry to-raise-children

           οἰκοδεσποτεῖν, μηδεμίαν ἀφορμὴν διδόναι
           to-master-household no occasion to-give

           τῷ ἀντικειμένῳ λοιδορίας χάριν·
           to-the opponent slander on-account-of

           'So I would have younger widows marry, bear children, rule their households, and give the enemy no occasion to revile us.'

      15 ἤδη γάρ τινες ἐξετράπησαν ὀπίσω τοῦ Σατανᾶ.
           already for some have-turned-away after the Satan

'For some have already strayed after Satan.'

In 1 Tim. 5:11a Paul says to Timothy νεωτέρας ... χήρας παραιτοῦ 'refuse to enroll younger widows'. In 11b–13 he gives the reason for such a directive, listing some of the problems enrolling them would entail. Then in v. 14, with οὖν, Paul resumes his directive regarding young widows. He directs that they remarry and live exemplary lives. Guthrie (1957:104) considers v. 14 to be a continuation of the preceding section in the sense that it is an inference, as his translation 'therefore' indicates. (Nearly all the commentators consider οὖν to be inferential in this context.) Even though the context is indeed resumptive, οὖν also has inferential force; that is, it draws a conclusion from the supportive material introduced by γάρ.

A similar structure is in 2 Tim. 1:6–8:

2 Tim. 1:6 δι' ἥν   αἰτίαν ἀναμιμνῄσκω σε ἀναζωπυρεῖν
            for which reason I-remind   you to-rekindle

τὸ χάρισμα   τοῦ   θεοῦ, ὅ   ἐστιν ἐν σοὶ
the gracious-gift of-the God   which is   in you

διὰ   τῆς ἐπιθέσεως τῶν   χειρῶν μου·
through the laying-on of-the hands of-me

'Hence I remind you to rekindle the gift of God that is within you through the laying on of my hands.'

7 οὐ **γὰρ** ἔδωκεν ἡμῖν ὁ θεὸς πνεῦμα δειλίας,
  not for   he-gave to-us the God spirit of-fear

ἀλλὰ δυνάμεως καὶ ἀγάπης καὶ σωφρονισμοῦ
but   of-power and of-love and of-moderation

'for God did not give us a spirit of timidity but a spirit of power and love and self-control.'

8 μὴ **οὖν** ἐπαισχυνθῇς   τὸ μαρτύριον τοῦ κυρίου ἡμῶν
  not oὖν   you-be-ashamed the testimony of-the Lord of-us

μηδὲ ἐμὲ τὸν δέσμιον αὐτοῦ, ἀλλὰ συγκακοπάθησον
nor me the prisoner of-him but suffer-evil-with

τῷ   εὐαγγελίῳ κατὰ   δύναμιν θεοῦ
for-the gospel   according-to power   of-God

'Do not be ashamed then of testifying to our Lord, nor of me his prisoner, but share in suffering for the gospel in the power of God,'

In 2 Tim. 1:6 Paul encourages his young co-worker to use the gift God has given him. With γάρ he presents the reason for his encouragement (v. 7). After this background information, Paul resumes with οὖν, drawing the inference for Timothy of what he just said. Since God gave Timothy the spirit of power, love, and self-discipline, "Paul can 'therefore' (οὖν) admonish Timothy not to 'be ashamed', i.e., embarrassed" (Knight 1992:372). Guthrie (1957:127) understands οὖν inferentially also, translating it 'therefore'. Most commentators cited by Minor (1992:18) indicate that the majority of the authors whom he cites take οὖν to be inferential in this context. I too conclude that even though the context is resumptive, οὖν has inferential force here.

The same is true of οὖν in 1 Tim. 2:8:

1 Tim. 2:3 τοῦτο καλὸν καὶ ἀπόδεκτον ἐνώπιον τοῦ σωτῆρος ἡμῶν θεοῦ,
this good and acceptable before the savior of-us God

'This is good, and is acceptable in the sight of God our Savior,'

4 ὃς παντας ἀνθρώπους θέλει σωθῆναι
who all people wishes to-be-saved

καὶ εἰς ἐπίγνωσιν ἀληθείας ἐλθεῖν.
and to knowledge of-truth to-come

'who desires all men to be saved and to come to the knowledge of the truth.'

5 εἷς **γὰρ** θεός, εἷς καὶ μεσίτης θεοῦ
one <u>for</u> God one also mediator of-God

καὶ ἀνθρώπων, ἄνθρωπος Χριστὸς Ἰησοῦς,
and people man Christ Jesus

'For there is one God, and there is one mediator between God and men, the man Christ Jesus,'

6 ὁ δοὺς ἑαυτὸν ἀντίλυτρον
the having-given himself payment

ὑπὲρ πάντων, τὸ μαρτύριον καιροῖς ἰδίοις·
for all the witness at.times private

'who gave himself as a ransom for all, the testimony to which was borne at the proper time.'

7 εἰς ὃ ἐτέθην ἐγὼ κῆρυξ καὶ ἀπόστολος,
into which I-was-placed myself herald and apostle

ἀλήθειαν λέγω, οὐ ψεύδομαι,
truth I-speak not I-lie

διδάσκαλος ἐθνῶν ἐν πίστει καὶ ἀληθείᾳ.
teacher of-Gentiles in faith and truth

'For this I was appointed a preacher and an apostle (I am telling the truth, I am not lying), a teacher of the Gentiles in faith and truth.'

8 Βούλομαι **οὖν** προσεύχεσθαι τοὺς ἄνδρας ἐν παντὶ τόπῳ,
I-want <u>οὖν</u> to-pray the men in every place

ἐπαίροντας ὁσίους χεῖρας χωρὶς ὀργῆς καὶ διαλογισμοῦ.
lifting-up   holy   hands without anger and doubt

'I desire then that in every place the men should pray, lifting holy hands without anger or quarreling;'

In 1 Tim. 2:1–2 Paul upholds the primacy of prayer. Then in vv. 3–4 Paul seems to digress, describing God's desire to save all people. In vv. 5–7 he gives background information introduced by γάρ, describing what God did through Jesus Christ to carry out this desire and how Paul himself was involved. Then in v. 8, with οὖν he resumes speaking about prayer, urging God's people to pray for all in authority, so that God's people may be able to live out the new life. Guthrie (1957:73) calls attention to the resumptive nature of οὖν: "Paul now resumes the subject of prayer." Most other commentators see οὖν as resumptive. But a close reading of the text reveals that more than resumption is involved. Knight (1992:127) picks this up: "Paul introduces his summary exhortation with 'therefore' (οὖν), pointing back again to the preceding argument as the warrant for his charge." Thus while the context is primarily resumptive, inference is present as well in v. 8, which is the case whenever the "interruption" is supportive material introduced by γάρ.

7.5 Conclusion

Since οὖν is inferential both when there is no interruption in the argument and also when a topic is resumed following an interruption introduced by γάρ, I conclude that the basic function of οὖν is inferential. This basic function is sometimes weakened, so that inferential appears in the subset of resumption.

8 Conclusion

In the pastoral epistles all the conjunctions as well as adverbial καί function very much the same as in Classical Greek, even though the uses may be somewhat different in certain respects. In my efforts to ascertain this, some of the classical grammarians were more helpful than others. Denniston almost invariably pointed me in the right direction. Smyth and BDR were next in being helpful. Liddell and Scott and BAGD often left me in a quandary. Though they provided a summary, their categories did not always match it. It was only with the help of other reference works and my adviser, that I could make sense of them.

Following Denniston's lead and applying Leech's (1983) position to conjunctions, I hold that each conjunction has one basic function, even though their uses are varied. In fact, the implications of their presence can change markedly, according to the context. The translator and interpreter must take every occurrence of a conjunction seriously and try to understand it in its own context, while keeping the basic function in mind.

The following is a summary of my conclusions regarding each of the conjunctions as well as the adverbial καί in the order in which they have been treated in the book.

Ἀλλά as a marker of contrast

Both traditional and discourse linguists recognize ἀλλά as an adversative (i.e., opposing) particle with a basic function of contrast. The presence of a negative affects the meaning of the conjunction. When the first conjunct is negated, ἀλλά introduces a second conjunct which replaces the rejected proposition. When the conjunct in which ἀλλά appears is negated, the conjunction ἀλλά denies the expectations raised by the preceding conjunct. In the absence of a negative, the second proposition corrects expectations introduced by the first one. In the set construction οὐ μόνον ... ἀλλὰ καί, ἀλλά functions in the same way as it does elsewhere.

Γάρ as a marker of confirmation

While traditional classical Greek linguists claim that conjunctive γάρ is confirmatory, introducing a proposition which is either causal or explanatory, traditional New Testament scholars note the preponderance of causal use. Discourse linguists call attention to the function of γάρ as a background marker, providing either confirmation or support for a previous proposition or assumption. Some of them describe its function as explanatory; others hold it to be causal. In the pastoral epistles the basic function of γάρ is to introduce propositions which confirm and strengthen a preceding conjunct, usually one that immediately precedes. In its specific uses it can indicate reason and sometimes also explanation.

Δέ as a marker of development

Traditional scholars maintain that δέ has two basic functions, contrastive and copulative. Even so, they themselves indicate that the contrastive function is basic and that δέ functions in a copulative fashion only when no difference exists between the two clauses which it joins. Most discourse linguists agree with this. From my analysis of the pastoral epistles, however, my conclusion is that neither "contrastive" nor "copulative" captures the function of δέ. Rather, δέ marks development. If δέ introduces a copulative proposition, it marks development from one proposition to another. If it introduces a contrastive proposition, it builds on the preceding conjunct as a foil, as it makes its distinctive contributions to the proposition prior to the foil. Even in set constructions, δέ does not lose its basic developmental function. In some sense, it is always developmental.

Adverbial καί as a marker of addition

Throughout the pastoral epistles the basic function of adverbial καί is to mark the word, phrase, or clause which immediately follows it for parallel processing with a corresponding constituent stated or implied in an earlier proposition. Καί is never correctly classified as pleonastic (i.e., redundant). Rather, as Denniston claims, the additive function is primary.

Conjunctive καί as a marker of addition

Whether adverbial or conjunctive, the basic function of καί is additive. It associates the material which it introduces with contiguous material. It has an additive, not a developmental, function. Καί can join formally equal or formally unequal constituents. When doubt arises about the function of καί, the context will usually help determine whether it is conjunctive or adverbial. In a correlative construction the second καί functions as a marker of addition between (generally) contiguous constituents while the first one marks for parallel processing. Whereas ellipsis usually occurs when καί is present, prepositions and determiners are repeated when the constituents concerned are to be viewed as individual entities.

Οὖν as a marker of inference

The adverbial function of οὖν present in Classical Greek disappeared before the time of the New Testament. What survived was οὖν as an inferential and resumptive conjunction. The function of οὖν does not appear to change when it is used in conjunction with other particles; it still marks either inference or continuation. The basic function of the conjunctive οὖν is inference. This function is found even in resumptive contexts, though it may be weakened to a continuative use, as an earlier topic is resumed and further developed.

The results of this investigation support Leech's (1983) advocacy for "complementarism." When we approach the study of the particles from the point of view of their each having various uses, we may be faithful to the facts, but we lose the center that holds them together. We will have the luxuriant growth of a tropical forest with the profusion of branches, leaves, and color, but without order and usefulness. On the other hand, when we approach the particles from the point of view that each has a singular function, but without taking into account the multiplicity of their uses, we lose the richness and variety of their application. If, each time a particle occurs, it can only be translated one way, the landscape becomes drab, monotonic, and nearly lifeless. The middle road is complementarism, affording both the richness and variety, on the one hand, and simplicity and generality, on the other.

REFERENCES

acCordance. 1994. Deerfield, Ill: Gramcord Institute.
Aland, K., M. Black, C. M. Martini, B. M. Metzger, and A. Wikgren, eds. 1983. *The Greek New Testament.* 3d ed.(corrected). London: United Bible Societies.
The American Heritage Dictionary. 1982. Boston: Houghton Mifflin.
Banker, J. 1987. *A Semantic Structure Analysis of Titus.* Dallas: Summer Institute of Linguistics.
Barnhart, C. L., and Jess Stein. 1958. *The American College Dictionary.* New York: Random House.
Bauer, Wilhelm, W. F. Arndt, F. W. Gingrich, and F. Danker. 1979. *A Greek-English Lexicon of the Writings of the New Testament and Other Early Christian Literature.* Chicago: University of Chicago Press.
Bernard, J. H. 1906. *The Pastoral Epistles.* Cambridge: University Press.
Black, D. A., ed. 1992. *Linguistics and New Testament Interpretation.* Nashville: Broadman Press.
Blass, Friederich, A. Debrunner, and F. Rehkopf. 1976. *Grammatik des neutestametlichen Griechisch.* Göttingen: Vandenhoeck and Ruprecht.
Blass, Regina. 1993. "Constraints on Relevance in Koine Greek in the Pauline Epistles." Paper presented at the Exegetical Seminar in Nairobi, Kenya, May 29 to June 19. Summer Institute of Linguistics.
Brown, Roy. 1988. macBible 2.0. Grand Rapids: Zondervan Electronic Publishing.
Buth, Randall. 1981. "Semitic 'kai' and Greek 'de'." *Selected Technical Articles Related to Translation* 3:12–19. Dallas: Summer Institute of Linguistics.
———. 1991. "'And' or 'but', so what?" *Jerusalem Perspective* 4(2):13–15 (March–April).
———. 1992. "Οὖν, Δέ, Καί, and Asyndeton in John's Gospel." In *Linguistics and New Testament Interpretation,* pp. 144–61. *See* Black 1992.
Callow, Kathleen. 1992. "The Disappearance of δέ in 1 Corinthians." In *Linguistics and New Testament Interpretation,* pp. 183–93. *See* Black 1992.
Denniston, John D. 1954. *The Greek Particles.* Oxford: Clarendon Press.
Edwards, B. B. 1993. "The Genuineness of the Pastoral Epistles." *Bibliotheca Sacra* 150:131–39.
Goddard, Jean. 1977. "Some Thoughts on δέ and καί in Acts 5:1–81a." *Translation Department Microfiche Library* 12:79227. Dallas: Summer Institute of Linguistics.
Graham, Glenn. 1976. "Exegetical Helps on the First Epistle to Timothy." Mimeo. (Unpublished.)
Guthrie, Donald. 1957. *The Pastoral Epistles.* The Tyndale New Testament Commentaries. Grand Rapids: Eerdmans.
Harbeck, W. 1970. "Mark's Use of *gar* in Narration." *Notes on Translation* 38:10–15.
Hodge, Charles. 1859. *An Exposition of the Second Epistle to the Corinthians.* Grand Rapids: Eerdmans.
Knight, George W. 1992. *Commentary on the Pastoral Epistles.* Grand Rapids: Eerdmans.

Kühner, Raphael, and Gernhard Gerth. 1955. *Ausführliche Grammatik der griechischen Sprache.* 2 vols. Leverkusen: Gottschalksche Verlagsbuchhandlung.

Larsen, I. 1991. "Notes on the Function of γάρ, οὖν, μέν, δέ, καί, and τέ in the Greek New Testament." *Notes on Translation* 5(1):35–47.

Leech, Geoffrey N. 1983. *Principles of Pragmatics.* London: Longman.

Levinsohn, Stephen H. 1977. "The Function of δέ in the Narrative of Mark 14:1–16:8. *Notes on Translation* 66:19–28.

———. 1979. "Four Narrative Connectives in the Acts of the Apostles." *Notes on Translation* 69:1–20.

———. 1980. "Relationships between Constituents beyond the Clause in the Acts of the Apostles." Ph.D. diss., University of Reading.

———. 1981. "Sentence Conjunctions and Development Units in the Narrative of Acts." *Selected Technical Articles Related to Translation* 5:2–39. Dallas: Summer Institute of Linguistics.

———. 1987. *Textual Connections in Acts.* Atlanta: Scholars Press.

———. 1992. *Discourse Features of New Testament Greek: A Coursebook.* Dallas: Summer Institute of Linguistics.

Liddell, Henry G., and Robert Scott. [1897] 1940. *A Greek-English Lexicon.* Rev. ed. Oxford: Clarendon.

———. 1889. *An Intermediate Greek-English Lexicon.* Oxford: Clarendon.

Lock, Walter. 1924. *A Critical and Exegetical Commentary on the Pastoral Epistles.* New York: Charles Scribner's.

Mann, William C., and Sandra A. Thompson. 1987. *Antithesis: A Study in Clause Ordering and Discourse Structure.* Marina del Rey, Calif.: Information Sciences Institute.

macBible. 1988. See Brown 1988.

Minor, Eugene E. 1992. *An Exegetical Summary of 2 Timothy.* Dallas: Summer Institute of Linguistics.

Moulton, James H., and Nigel Turner. 1963. *A Grammar of New Testament Greek,* vol. 3. Edinburgh: T & T. Clark.

Nestle, Eberhard, K. Aland, M. Black, C. M. Martini, B. M. Metzger, and A. Wikgren. 1979. *Novum Testamentum Graece.* Stuttgart: Deutsche Bibelgesellschaft.

New American Standard Bible. 1985. Nashville: Thomas Nelson.

Poythress, Vern S. 1984. "The Use of the Intersentence Conjunctions DE, OUN, KAI, and Asyndeton in the Gospel of John." *Novum Testamentum* 20:312–40.

Reimer, M. 1985. "The Function of οὖν in the Gospel of John." *Selected Technical Articles Related to Translation* 13:28–36. Dallas: Summer Institute of Linguistics.

Revised Standard Version. 1971. New York: American Bible Society.

Robinson, Edward. 1855. *A Greek-English Lexicon of the New Testament.* New York: Harper.

Robson, Edward A. [1979] 1980. (This 1979 dissertation was revised by the author in May 1980. "Kai-Configuration in the Greek New Testament." Ph.D. diss., Syracuse University.

Schwyzer, Eduard, and Albert Debrunner. 1950. *Griechische Grammatik.* Munich: Beck'sche Verlagsbuchhandlung.

Smyth, Herbert W. 1956. *Greek Grammar.* Cambridge, Mass.: Harvard University Press.

Titrud, Kermit. 1986. "The Abused Kai." M.A. thesis, Trinity Evangelical Divinity School, Deerfield, Illinois.

———. 1991. "The Overlooked Καί in the Greek New Testament." *Notes on Translation* 5(1):1–28.

———. 1992. "The Function of Καί in the Greek New Testament and an Application to 2 Peter." In *Linguistics and New Testament Interpretation,* pp. 240–70. See Black 1992.

Travis, Edna J. 1972. *Exegetical Helps on Second Timothy.* A Private Publication.

Winer, Georg B. 1877. *A Treatise on the Grammar of New Testament Greek.* Edinburgh: T. & T. Clark.

ISBN 1-55671-041-0

www.ingramcontent.com/pod-product-compliance
Lightning Source LLC
Chambersburg PA
CBHW051815230426
43672CB00012B/2741